ESSENTIALS OF NURSING MANAGEMENT

Communication Skills

Barbara Scammell

MACMILLAN

1715375

First published 1990 by
THE MACMILLAN PRESS LTD
Houndmills, Basingstoke, Hampshire RG21 2XS
and London
Companies and representatives
throughout the world

ISBN 0–333–48567–X

A catalogue record for this book is available
from the British Library.

Printed in Hong Kong

Reprinted 1991, 1992

Contents

Acknowledgements

I should like to thank Jill Baker and Mary Waltham for their help, advice and patience. It was a delight to work with them.

I should also like to thank David Sines and Sheila Marson for the most helpful editorial comments they offered, which I was very grateful to receive.

To my husband and my son I am indebted for unstinting support and encouragement.

During the writing of this book I sought the help of my local hospital, The Royal Treliske Hospital, Truro, and I should like to thank the Sisters, Charge Nurses and Student Nurses who allowed me to be a 'fly on the wall' in their wards and units. Special thanks are due to Mrs Weston, District Nursing Officer, and Ms Chapman, Senior Nurse Manager at Treliske, who gave me so much of their valuable time. It was an experience that renewed my pride in having been, for so many years, part of a noble and deeply caring profession, and it gave me encouragement to find that, whatever the ills of the NHS, love, gentleness and compassion continue to motivate my Brothers and Sisters in nursing as they always have. I should like to make it clear that none of the cases cited in Chapters 7 and 8 were observed at Treliske.

Barbara Scammell

The author and publishers wish to thank the following who have kindly given permission for the use of copyright material: Harper & Row Publishers, Inc. for a chart from *Motivation and Personality* by Abraham H. Maslow. Copyright 1954 by Harper & Row Publishers, Inc. Copyright ©1970 by Abraham H. Maslow; Heinemann Professional Publishing Ltd for material from *Manager Teams: Why They Succeed or Fail* by R. Meredith Belbin, 1984; Neil Rackham for material from *Behaviour Analysis in Training* by Neil Rackham and Terry Morgan, McGraw-Hill Book Company (UK) Ltd, 1977.

Every effort has been made to trace all the copyright holders, but if any have been inadvertently overlooked the publishers will be pleased to make the necessary arrangement at the first opportunity.

Preface

Ralph Waldo Emerson said 'It is a luxury to be understood.' Peter Drucker, the doyen of management theory, claimed that 'good management begins with good communication'. If both these sentiments contain even a kernel of truth, how can they be reconciled?

The theory expressed in this book rests on the notion that good communication can be learned and improved, and that it begins with good listening and a preparedness to acknowledge the ideas, ideals, morals, mores and ethics of others, while at the same time considering the adaptation of one's own to suit changing circumstances, or because one has been shown that they are unacceptable to others.

The prime purpose of eloquence should be to express oneself clearly and unambiguously and not, as Louis Vermeil postulated, to keep other people from speaking!

As the famous philosopher Anon. said, 'The older I get, the less I say and the more I listen to and observe others.' While age is not a criterion of maturity, experience, gained by he who will profit by it, may be.

In this book we are doing more than talking about talking. We are considering how we communicate, and how communication can make us better people, and, specifically, better managers.

John Adair[1] described three areas of leadership (see Figure 1). Following his model the three areas of communication described in this book are shown in Figure 2. These areas are indivisible and interlocking. They describe, in Part I of the book, the psychology and skills of communication in society generally; in Part II they relate these skills to the tasks of management; and in Part III consideration is given to some of the areas of nurse management which offer examples of practice at the level of delivery of care, and suggest areas and issues needing particular study.

Figure 1

The material in this book is intended to advance the thesis that the competent accomplishment of management tasks depends on well-developed communications and sensitive, accurate and appropriate communicating.

The way the material is presented lends itself to:

- use in training schools or other training centres
- distance learning

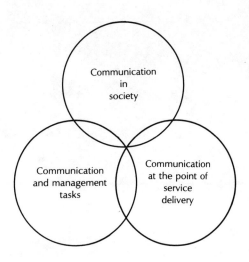

Figure 2

- use as a reference book and checklist to assist in the improvement of management techniques.

Failures in every area of human society can, in general, be traced back to a lack of adequate communication.

The most important, and the least well-used skill of communicating, is that of accurate listening and attending.

Every manager should therefore become an excellent communicator and an obsessional listener!

As the topics raised here are closely linked, so are all the books in the series. 'Know thyself' is the basic message of the first, and the basis upon which all the following books are built.

It is hoped that in this book the exercises suggested will enable this basic ability to be realised, so that the student who is in search of a better management style may be enabled to achieve it. To do this is not an easy practice, but it is one that will offer rich rewards in its accomplishment.

Reference

1. John Adair, *Effective leadership, a self development manual* (Aldershot: Gower, 1983).

Part I   The Basics and Range of Communications

Part I of the book deals with the bricks and mortar of communications and communicating, asking such questions as **Why? How? When?** and **What?** do we communicate.

Chapter 1   Communication in society

To understand how communication is used in society, it is helpful to consider:

- why we communicate
- how we communicate
- what interferes with accurate communication
- what are the main components of the personality that influences communication.

Why do we communicate?

If we consider the Hierarchy of Human Needs, suggested by Maslow,[1] it is possible to associate a form of communication with each category of human need or drive (see Table 1), and it becomes apparent that at some point in our lives we use every category of communication to satisfy one or other of our human needs.

Exercise 1

The following exercise is designed to help identify the reasons why communication takes place in human interaction.

Verbal communications are used:

 (1) to conduct social interaction
 (2) to act as a vehicle of change
 (3) to attempt to influence others
 (4) to instruct, teach or educate
 (5) to issue orders
 (6) to warn
 (7) to exchange thoughts or ideas
 (8) to express feelings and emotions
 (9) to help or seek help
(10) to persuade or negotiate.

Into which category do the following sentences fall? Signify by using the numbers (1)–(10).

(a) 'I think we should consider closing this ward in the interests of economy.'
(b) 'It's very good to meet you again.'
(c) 'When my mother died, I was very upset for a long time. I couldn't get over it.'
(d) 'If you will agree to work week ends, we will look for ways of increasing staffing at difficult times.'
(e) 'I have found that it is useful to employ this technique. You might wish to try it.'
(f) 'Go and collect the report from Dr Jones, please.'
(g) 'Can you ask Mr Price to come and look at this patient please?'
(h) 'I would like to see if we could improve this procedure by simplifying it.'
(i) 'All specimens, when they have been collected, must be correctly labelled and left here for collection.'
(j) 'It is very dangerous to allow patients to smoke in the ward. Not only is oxygen used here, but there are other reasons. Can you tell me what they are?'

Answers on page 11.

Table 1 Categories of human drives and associated categories of communication

Category of drives	Drives	Associated category of communication

1 Physiological drives	Food
	Rest
	Shelter
	Sex
		To teach the young:
		  how to get food
		  how to build a shelter
		To co-operate in 'nest' building
		To express sexual needs and obtain consent to mutual sexual expression

2 Security drives	Protection from:
	  threat
	  danger
	  deprivation
		To teach the young:
		  what is dangerous
		  how to avoid danger
		To warn the 'tribe' of danger
		To express and demonstrate loving and caring emotions to prevent deprivation – particularly in the young

3 Social drives	Belonging – peer groups, social groups Giving and receiving friendship Giving and receiving love	To exhibit appropriate inter-personal skills which will ensure acceptance in the group To demonstrate social skills To express emotions – love, pleasure, fear, anger, etc. To help and to seek help
4 Ego drives (self-esteem)	Self-respect Self-confidence Autonomy Competence Achievement	To demonstrate (verbally and non-verbally) status, confidence and achievement To demonstrate competence in living and in work To demonstrate self-confidence

5 Ego drives
   (esteem of others)
	Reputation shown by:
	  status
	  recognition
	  appreciation
	  respect
		To teach and educate
		To issue orders, manage and control others
		To influence, persuade and negotiate
		To act as a vehicle of change
		To demonstrate ability, competence and a right to respect

6 Self-fulfillment (self-actualisation)	Realising potential Self-development Creativity	To teach and educate To express and exchange thoughts, ideas and ideals To consider moral and theological questions To communicate by painting, drawing, music and other art forms

How do we communicate?

1. By direct verbal communication

The manner in which verbal communication occurs can best be described diagrammatically (see Figure 3).

- The speaker can be in communication with **one** person or many.
- At each stage there can be interference with the communication which can distort or change it.

2. By indirect verbal communication

When an instrument is used to transmit messages, communication is subject to distortion. The 'instrument' may be a mechanical object, such as a telephone, or the voice of a messenger. The latter is probably the least reliable as the thoughts of the human 'instrument' are also involved.

3. By writing

Those who manage others will be required to communicate in writing in addition to using verbal communication. A well-written, easily assimilated document is a permanent record of the writer's thoughts, findings or requests. Assembled and arranged to appeal to the reader, it can be invaluable. Communication in writing can be presented in many different forms.

3.1 Reports
- Daily or long-term reports of patients' progress. These are or can be used as legal documents and must be **clear** and **unequivocal.**

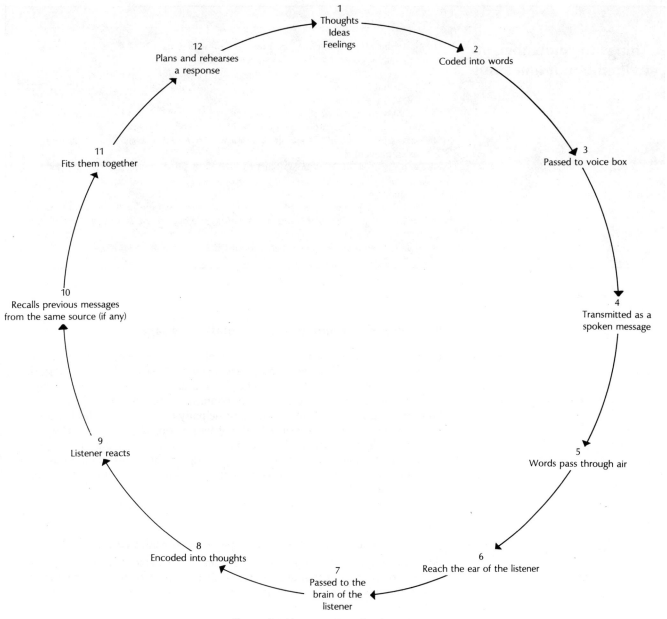

Figure 3 How communication occurs

- Reports provided to investigate standards of care, to report on progress of some kind or to make the case for more resources.
- Statistical reports.

3.2 Appraisals and references: assessments

As these affect the future career of a person, they must be **objective, honest** and **just.** Because they are of such importance, Chapter 5 is devoted to them.

3.3 Instructions for treatment

It is especially vital that these are clear, unambiguous and easily read. All those using such instructions must be prepared to check if there is any doubt as to the meaning.

3.4 Requests for equipment and stores

These too must be clear, unambiguous and easily read, and there should be no doubt as to their meaning.

4. By the 'grape vine'

Do not despise your grape vine, but do not act on it either! Use it as a means of testing the water and of seeking trends in behaviour and opinion. **Check it out.**

<table>
<tr><td>

Things to remember in written communication

</td><td>

(1) All writing should be **clear** and **concise.** Do not try to use long, 'literary' words, especially if you are not sure what they mean!
(2) Before embarking on a piece of written communication, ask yourself:
   (a) What is it's purpose?
   (b) Who is it for?
   (c) What do you want to achieve by it?
(3) Always write a rough outline before writing the finished piece.
(4) Make sure the writing is **legible.** Writing was invented to **assist** communication, not to **prevent** it.
(5) Do not be ashamed of 'going back to school' to brush up on your writing skills. Most of us have been away from school for a long time, and our skills need polishing!
(6) Try to avoid jargon unless you are certain that the reader(s) will understand it.
(7) Try to find out what the reader(s) want from the document and balance your needs with theirs.
(8) Always keep a variety of reference books beside you when writing.

</td></tr>
</table>

5. By non-verbal communication (body language)

Before an exchange of words has taken place, the two people engaged in the exchange will have made a rough assessment of each other by categorizing each other into stereotypical sets. This assessment continues during the subsequent verbal exchange and may confirm or change the initial assessment. Stereotyping is useful in many ways, principally because it enables the observer to decide on his or her response to the other person, and may be vital when it is a case of 'flight or fight'. It is a purely animal reaction based on previous knowledge, experience or 'tribal' teaching. It becomes dangerous when, without reason, a stereotype is maintained which is not appropriate to the person observed.

Non-verbal communication operates in a number of different ways.

5.1 Proxemics – a study of the use of space in communicating

All animals guard their territorial space and their personal space.

Territorial space is that area within which a person operates and which is his or her family's alone. This is usually a dwelling place. Within the dwelling place, there are rooms into which others are invited to enter for certain, usually social, purposes, and there are rooms, such as the bedrooms, which are not usually accessible to others. This is important when a visitor, such as a District Nurse, a Health Visitor or a Doctor, calls on a household. Normally such people are invited to enter the living room, a privilege that they must respect. A District Nurse and a Doctor may also be required to enter the 'inner sanctum' of the bedroom, which is an even greater privilege.

Personal space is an invisible distance around us within which we function and which we prefer others **not** to enter. The constant invasion of personal space has been cited as one cause of aggression in crowded city areas.

<table>
<tr><td>

Exercise 2

</td><td>

Observe what happens when:

(1) In an almost empty cafe, where there are many empty seats, you choose to sit at a table already occupied by one other person.
(2) You press too closely to someone in a queue. Watch how people behave:
   (a) in a crowded lift
   (b) when entering an empty tube train that subsequently fills up. Where do people choose to sit first? What 'barriers' do they erect?
(3) Desmond Morris[2] claims that different races maintain different distances between people when engaged in conversation. Observe, in the street, at parties or on television, whether you can differentiate between races by their behaviour (touching, etc.) and by their observance of personal space.

</td></tr>
</table>

5.2 Kinesics – the description of visual behaviour

Visual behaviour is often determined by race, culture or social status. Italians are said to 'talk with their hands', although there are many Italians who do not behave in this way!

In addition to racial stereotypes, everyone develops his or her own set of body movements which, to an onlooker, provides clues to the person's emotional state and feelings. Status and social background can also be determined by body movements.

5.3 Appearance

The appearance of a person often provides clues to his or her social status, lifestyle and background. It also provides some clue to the emotional state of the person. Dress, ornamentation, make up and hair style all contribute to the impression the wearer seeks to make. In addition we observe height and weight, and the cumulative data gives us a stereotype concept of who and what the person represents to us. Many races are, of course, instantly recognised by their colour or features, and this leads to a stereotyped picture which is not only determined by our previous personal experience, but may also be coloured by prejudice.

5.4 Environmental messages

In this picture which we build up about those we meet, much may be gleaned from houses, furniture and other artifacts with which people surround themselves. From them we learn whether a person has similar tastes to ourselves, whether a person is ostentatious in his or her choice and use of such artifacts, or whether a person seeks conformity to a group or social set.

5.5 Touch

This is a delicate and potentially dangerous intrusion into another individual's personal space. Some people are prepared to touch and be touched, while others detest such close contact. The necessity for nurses to touch and perform intimate tasks for virtual strangers puts them and their patients into an invidious position, and may lead to a confrontational relationship giving rise to resentment and anger. On the other hand, an arm round the shoulders of a grieving relative or a frightened patient can bring solace and a release of tension.

The use of touch requires delicacy of feeling and sensitivity.

Functions of non-verbal communication	(1) It acts as a symbolic message.
	(2) It can define race, culture and social status.
	(3) It signals relational communication in the areas of attraction, credibility, dislike and so forth.
	(4) It establishes roles between communicators by determining who speaks first, who acts as the leader of the dialogue and who is the dominant personality.
	(5) It helps to regulate the flow of conversation, thereby enabling interaction.
	(6) It acts as a form of self-preservation through the recognition of potential danger.
	(7) It reinforces verbal interaction and thus aids learning of attitude and behaviour change.

6. Paralanguage

This does not properly belong to either verbal or non-verbal communication. It indicates the tone of voice and other variations in speech, and it affects and reinforces the verbal messages being transmitted.

What interferes with accurate communication?

Looking at Figure 3 it is obvious that communication is a complicated process and that there must be a number of points at which the accuracy of the communication is vulnerable.

When verbal communication takes place, interference occurs at almost every stage of the model:

- **Step 1:** Thoughts, ideas and feelings are initially a jumble of electrical impulses, leaping across the synapses of the brain's neurones in response to its impressions and bodily needs. Any impairment of the brain itself caused through alcohol, drugs, injury or age, for example, can interfere with the accurate transfer of these impulses.
- **Step 2:** When thoughts are coded into words, the ability to express them accurately and clearly will be affected if the speaker is inarticulate, lacks clarity of thought or speaks in an unfamiliar language.
- **Step 4:** The coded message is next transmitted as the spoken word. There may be a lack of clarity of speech due to:
  − a speech impediment
  − a heavy accent
  − too rapid or too slow delivery
  − using long, involved sentences
  − using jargon or words not understood by the listener
  − making contradictory statements or changing instructions in the course of one exchange
  − mumbling or speaking very quietly.
- **Step 5:** We are all only too familiar with the noise pollution of the air and, as our words pass through air, they can be masked by the sound of aeroplanes, loud music, others speaking and a multitude of other external noises.
- **Step 6:** When the speaker's words reach the ear of the listener(s), he or she may be:
  − speaking to the wrong person
  − speaking to someone with imperfect hearing
  − speaking to someone who is not listening or who is listening imperfectly.
- **Step 7:** The message, in its passage to the brain of the listener, encounters several barriers:
  − the listener may have imperfectly understood or heard, but be afraid to interrupt to say so
  − there may be a lack of interest in the communication which distracts the listener
  − the listener may be so distracted by his or her own affairs as to be unable to listen.
- **Step 8:** During the encoding process there could be accidental or deliberate misinterpretation of what was said.
- **Step 9:** The reaction of the listener will lead to a response of some kind.
- **Steps 10, 11, 12:** At this point the listener is recalling previous messages from the same source. The listener may be tempted to feel that he or she has heard it all before and 'switch off' in irritation. It is usually at such a point that the familiar message contains a new element which is missed!

During the latter part of an exchange the listener is often 'rehearsing' his or her response. This, added to the other 'brain noise' of impressions, thoughts and ideas flooding the mind, can result in the loss of some, if not all, of the message.

Main components of the personality that influences communication

Figure 4 explains in diagrammatic form how the persona affects the ability of a human being to communicate clearly and unambiguously.

1. Self concept

This is a central element of communication which is built from the values the person holds; his or her beliefs, attitudes and perceptions of the world and of those who inhabit it. The self concept, once created, is not a static entity. It can change, as beliefs, values and perceptions of the world change.

It is also influenced by the regard which others have for its owner and helps to maintain the owner's social and ego drives. The self concept also creates the way in which a person presents him or herself to the world, and offers the first clue as to the kind of communication which will be forthcoming from that

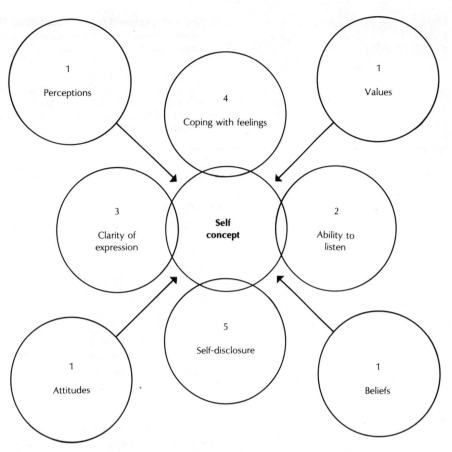

Figure 4   How self concept is built and influences communication

Based on: Mynon R. Chartier, 'Five components contributing to effective interpersonal communications' in *The 1974 Annual Handbook for Group Facilitators*, eds Pfeiffer & Jones (University Associates Inc.)

person. A positive self concept, for example, will lead to positive and confident interactions with others, while a weak uncertain concept of self leads to wavering and hesitant interactions.

2. Elements linked to self concept

2.1 Ability to listen

As a central skill of communication, this will be discussed in greater detail later. It is affected by such factors as a person's estimate of his or her own importance, which may make that person feel that there are few people worth listening to, or a lack of tolerance towards those with differing values.

Accurate listening is concerned with attending to **all** aspects of verbal and non-verbal communication, thus ensuring an accurate translation and understanding of the messages being transmitted.

2.2 Clarity of expression

This means:

● thinking clearly and logically
● speaking clearly and unambiguously
● expressing thoughts in a simple, easily understood manner[3].

Exercise 3

(1) Read a tax form or any form produced by a government department. Was it **easily** understandable? If not, what made it difficult to understand?
    (a) Use of difficult words?
    (b) Poor arrangement of sentences?
    (c) Other reasons?

(2) You wish to close a ward for upgrading. This will meet with some opposition from nurses and doctors and will cause disruption to other departments in the hospital. Write a **short** report which will:
   (a) Calm the situation.
   (b) Point out the advantages.
   (c) Convince people that it must be done.
Ask a colleague to read your report and comment on whether he or she has been convinced by your arguments. Point out that the only way you will learn is by **honest criticism.**

2.3 Coping with feelings

One of the most potent obstacles to the ability to comprehend the crux of other people's communications can be the feelings and emotions of the listener. These may take the listener by surprise. His or her reaction is to try to analyse them, to wonder with surprise why he or she feels that way, and thus to lose the drift of the communication which is continuing.

'Know thyself' is an important rule which the good communicator should observe, but self-knowledge is difficult to acquire. (To study this further, see the volume *Managing Yourself* in this series.)[4] Personal feelings and the personal moral and ethical stance are elements of the personality which, in the mature person, have been arrived at over a period of time and after intense contemplation. They will not be readily changed or abandoned, nor should they be. While they may be 'right' for one person, the unique character of every human being means that they may not be right for or acceptable to another. Moreover this does not make the person who dissents 'wrong'. His or her beliefs, attitudes and ethics must be respected. Mature people are able to control their feelings when listening to others, recognising the rights of others to hold their views.

While respecting the rights of others, one must also be confident in one's own right to respect and be prepared to give others feedback on how their attitudes affect you. The way in which feedback can be sensitively and effectively offered is discussed in Chapter 2.

2.4 Self-disclosure

The effective communicator should be secure enough to be able to disclose those feelings or ideas which will be of value to the exchange of thought, and add something to the communication.

Most people at some time have 'hidden agendas'; that is, goals they have in mind, which they do not reveal to others. In many communications they are necessary and acceptable. However, lack of maturity and self-confidence lead to secret and introverted attitudes, inappropriate to the occasion, or constant in nature, and these attitudes are damaging to the person who holds them, and to the organisation for whom that person works.

One block to self-disclosure is the individual's fear of criticism. Indeed, at times, and in situations where the climate is not one of trust and openness, it is wise **not** to indulge in public self-disclosure.

A failure to be open in one's behaviour goes further than a reluctance to disclose personal feelings. The person who feels that knowledge is power, and who therefore discloses little information, is frequently encountered. Such a person gains the reputation of 'sitting' on all reports, notices and other material meant for wide publication. In time, as the information fails to get passed on, it is no longer sent to that person. Not only does that person suffer as a result, but his or her subordinates also suffer through that person's reluctance to communicate.

2.5 Defence mechanisms

These will be discussed in Chapter 4.

The need for effective and efficient communications by managers

Koontz, O'Donnell and Weihrich[5] contend that 'Communication is essential for the internal functioning of enterprises because it integrates the managerial functions. Specifically communication is needed:

- to establish and disseminate goals of an enterprise
- to develop plans for their achievement
- to organise human and other resources in the most effective and efficient way
- to select, develop and appraise members of the organisation
- to lead, direct and motivate members of the organisation
- to control performance.'

The ensuing chapters of this book will consider, in greater detail, the specific tasks of nurse management, how they relate to these managerial functions and how the functions are affected by communication.

Hints for effective and efficient communications

(1) Wherever possible use face-to-face communication, particularly when a difficult message is being transmitted.
(2) It is usually helpful to **reinforce verbal communication by written communications.**
(3) Make sure the message has been **clearly understood.** Do **not** say 'Do you understand?' Say instead 'Can we go over what I have just told you in case I have left anything out?'
(4) Consider the personality of the listener and tailor the style of the message to suit him or her.

Exercise 4

Consider the reasons why communication takes place (see page 3) and then answer the following questions:

(1) How easy or difficult do you find it to meet new people?
... k of **one** change you would like to make in your work situation.
... How would you set about making such a change?
... o would you inform and how?
... would you gain the co-operation of those involved?
... you teach someone how to take and record a telephone call?
... wn all the steps involved in the process.
... ach step.
... y you would explain each step.
... u know if you had been effective in your instruction?
... your life which had special significance for you. Describe
... a friend.

... y activities are described as 'communicating',
... iter' communication of the receptionist, to the very
... echniques used by the therapeutic counsellor. These
... ribed as a continuum and are shown as a model in Figure 5.
... apter we will look at this range of communications and try to
... each stage functions, its purpose and its results.

Answers to Exercise

(a) (7)	(b) (1)	(c) (8)
(d) (10)	(e) (3) and (4)	(f) (5)
(g) (1)	(h) (2) and (3)	(i) (4)
(j) (4) and (6)		

References

1. A. Maslow, *Motivation and Personality* (New York: Harper & Row, 1970).
2. Desmond Morris, *Manwatching* (London: Jonathan Cape, 1977).
3. Sir Ernest Gowers, *The Complete Plain Words* (London: Pelican Books, 1982).
4. V. Tschudin and J. Schober, *Managing Yourself* (London: Macmillan, 1990).
5. H. Koonitz, C. O'Donnell and H. Weihrich, *Management* (London: McGraw-Hill, 1980).

Suggested further reading

Reference books

A good up-to-date dictionary is essential, e.g.: *The Collins English Dictionary*, New Edition (Collins, 1986).

Accurate spelling is essential. A useful book is: Christine Maxwell, *The Pergamon Dictionary of Perfect Spelling* (Wheaton, 1977). This is a quick reference book which gives the rules of spelling.

J. I. Rodale, *The Synonym Finder* (Rodale Press, 1979).

Joel Arnstein, *The International Dictionary of Graphic Symbols* (London: Century Publishing, 1983).

Whitaker's Almanack, Complete Edition. (This need not be bought yearly.)

Books about communications and communicating

Will Bridge and Jill Maclead-Clark, *Communication in Nursing Care* (London: HM + M, 1981).

Robert Bolton, *People Skills* (New Jersey: Prentice-Hall Inc., 1979).

S. H. Burton, *People and Communication*, Longman Business Education Series (London: Longman, 1980).

Margaret Wolff and Graham Collins, *Communicating at Work*, Nelson BEC Books (Nelson, 1982).

Chapter 2

The communications continuum: forms and skills

Introduction

If we accept the notion that there may be some form of communications continuum, based on the use of social, interactive and counselling skills, it could best be described diagrammatically as shown in Figure 5.

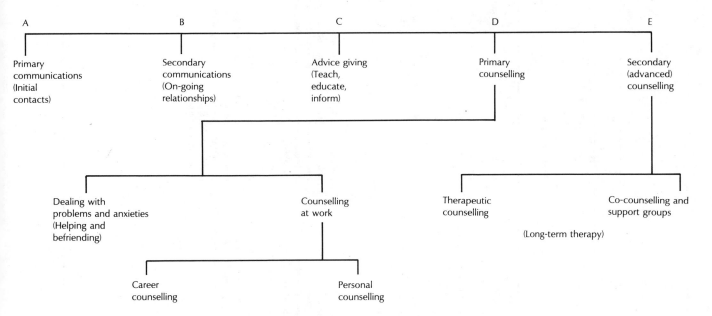

Figure 5 The communications continuum

The continuum can be expanded into a three-dimensional model which describes:

● the forms of communication used in the health service
● the skills attached to each stage of the continuum
● the staff who use the different stages of the continuum, and at which point (see Table 2).

1. Forms of communication

These are described in Figure 5. Generally nurse managers communicate in areas A, B, C and D. With the exception of those working in specialist fields, nurse managers do not function, or function very rarely, in area E, although they may use the associated skills. The exceptions will be considered later.

2. Skills used at each level

Attached to each area is a range of skills (see Table 2). Some of these skills are described as social or inter-personal skills, while others are specifically associated with the counselling end of the continuum.

Table 2 The communications continuum – related skills and who uses them

	A	B	C	D	D	E	E
	Primary communications	Secondary communications	Advice giving	Primary counselling	Counselling at work	Secondary counselling	Secondary counselling
				Problems and anxieties	Counselling at work	Therapeutic counselling	Co-counselling/support groups
1 Purpose	Initial contacts with others, 'shop window' encounters	On-going relationships: • verbal and non-verbal • written; Support groups (informal)	To offer factual information; To teach, instruct or supervise; To educate; Management coaching	To befriend those in need; To help others to problem solve; To befriend anyone who seeks such help	Career 'advice'; Possibly personal counselling; NB Not disciplinary	To give specific long-term help for: • drugs • alcohol • AIDS • marriage guidance, etc.	To help relieve the tensions in oneself and others caused by: • stressful work • counselling others
2 Given by	Everyone in the NHS, but there are those who have a special responsibility, e.g., receptionists, OPD and record clerks, appointments clerks, porters, etc.	All health care staff; All managers and supervisors	Doctors; Nurses, midwives and HVs; Tutors and teachers; Managers	All health care workers; Managers	All managers and supervisors	Trained counsellors or psychotherapists	Mutual support between those in a counselling situation
3 Given to	Everyone who contacts the NHS, especially: • patients • clients • relatives	Patients; Clients; Relatives; Subordinates; Peers	Patients; Clients; Relatives; General public; Subordinates; Peers	Anyone who seeks help unless their problem requires someone with greater counselling ability	Subordinates seeking counselling about careers and those with work-related problems	Clients seeking help or those referred	Mutual
4 Skills and knowledge needed	Simple inter-personal or social skills, e.g.: • ability to listen • patiently helping • ability to put people at ease • assertiveness	Use of inter-personal skills; Knowledge of human behaviour; Knowledge of how groups form and work; Ability to give and receive feedback; Interviewing skills	As for A4 and B4; When to give advice and when to withhold it; Knowledge of the subject involved; Teaching skills; Presentational skills: • lecturing • speech making	As for A4 and B4; Ability to listen in a non-judgemental manner and to help in problem solving; Assisting in change	When to offer help and when to refer to someone else; Assisting with change	As for A4, B4, C4 and D4; Advanced, accurate empathy; Self-disclosure; Risk taking; Contract making; Confrontation; Questioning; Concreteness and consistency	
5 Qualities needed	Respect for others; Warm, caring personality; Sincerity; Desire to help; Patience; Primary empathy	As for A5; Dependability; Ethical probity	As for A5 and B5; Humility	As for A5, B5 and C5	As for A5, B5 and C5	As for A5, B5, C5 and D5; Openness and preparedness to disclose and share; Self-knowledge	

14

The skills and qualities needed in primary and secondary communications (areas A–C) are discussed in this chapter while Chapter 3 is devoted to the subject of counselling (areas D and E). This is designed to demonstrate the importance of understanding fully what counselling is and, in the light of such understanding, deciding how far nurse managers are or should be involved in counselling.

<table>
<tr><td>

Issues to consider

</td><td>

(1) Some people, by virtue of their nature and nurture, are more skilled than others in their short- or long-term relationships.
(2) Communication/inter-personal/social/counselling skills can be:
    (a) **learned or acquired**
    (b) **improved or enhanced.**
(3) Alongside the skills are associated qualities which the person must possess in order to:
    (a) be able to learn or improve skills
    (b) wish to do so
    (c) be able to use the skills.
(4) In order to live a socially well-adjusted and well-integrated life the basic inter-personal and social skills must be developed. This usually happens in the socialisation process of early life. In the majority of people these skills can be improved.
(5) Improvement of skills can only take place if it is realised that it is necessary and desirable to do so, and by honest feedback from others which will reveal the areas where improvement is needed.

</td></tr>
</table>

3. The staff who use the different forms of communication

The range of skills is used by a variety of health care workers in a variety of situations (see Table 2).

Primary communications

In Table 2 initial contacts are described as 'shop window' encounters. They set the scene for many of the relationships between health care workers and the public, who present themselves as patients or clients, or relatives of patients or clients. Although it is sometimes possible to rectify bad, first impressions, this is usually difficult to do, and those who suffer from the atmosphere that has been created are rarely those who created it. Thus the stresses of a relationship can be badly influenced from the few words uttered by a harassed secretary, receptionist or nurse; from, in fact, the first person encountered. The impression made on others at first meetings cannot be too strongly stressed, as it is here that insensitivity, rudeness and impatience are all too often displayed when anxious or grieving people meet with pressurised staff.

The constant pressure of relating to a demanding public, who may themselves demonstrate a similar lack of these qualities, can blunt the sensibilities of the man or woman with the highest degree of patience and good will, and constant care is needed to avoid impatient responses.

1. Skills and knowledge needed in primary communications

1.1 Listening

There is no doubt that this is the **primary** skill in all communications. It is also, sadly, the skill least well exercised.

Isolated within our own lives and introspectively working out our own primary and ultimate causes inclines us towards egocentricity. It is difficult enough to arrive at a balanced compendium of ideals, ethics, morals and principles with which we are comfortable, without the added burden of opening up to the 'agendas' of others. This is especially true when these agendas may be very different to our own and may challenge ideas which we have identified as 'right' and have settled, at a price, within our conscious and unconscious mind. Every instinct urges us to cling to the known, the understood and the comfortable, and to believe that our cluster of values and principles is right.

This instinct for self-confidence and self-protection has three effects:

- It makes any changes in attitudes difficult to achieve.
- It gives the individual the feeling that he or she is only comfortable with those who think in a similar pattern, at least as far as 'important' issues are concerned.
- Far more fundamentally, however, it means that superficial listening becomes such a part of us that it is difficult to rise above our own 'thought noise' and attend to what others are **saying** verbally and **expressing** non-verbally.

Improving and developing listening skills

(1) Concentration is difficult to maintain for longer than 15 to 20 minutes. Try not to make a speech; give someone instructions or run a training session which lasts longer than this **without** a change of pace or method of communication.

(2) The middle part of a sentence is the part least well heard, yet it is the part that usually contains the message.

(3) Wide differences in value systems, age, education or vocabulary will make communication between people more difficult. Where they exist, concentrate even harder on getting it right.

Exercises, such as the following, can be used very effectively to:

- demonstrate poor listening skills
- improve listening skills.

Exercise 5

Listening checklist
Over the following week keep a diary of your listening habits and note the following:

(1) In a dialogue with another person how much of the talking do you normally do? All? $\frac{1}{2}$? $\frac{1}{3}$? Very little?

(2) Do you find yourself talking at the same time as another person? Never? Sometimes? Frequently?

(3) When talking to a person do you look: At your desk? Out of the window? Round the room? At the speaker?

(4) Do you focus on a point a speaker has made and wait impatiently for an opportunity to answer it?

(5) Do you have any irritating habits while listening to another, for example, clicking a pen, playing with jewelry, etc.?

(6) Think of someone you often talk to who has an irritating habit. What effect does it have on you?

(7) How often in the course of a conversation do you 'drift off' into thoughts of your own?

(8) How often do you give advice or say 'If I were you I would...?'

(9) In an interview do you make judgements or assessments of the interviewee while you are talking to him or her?

(10) Think of your colleagues. Which of them would you say were: Good listeners? Bad listeners? Why?

(11) When you meet a stranger, who knows most about the other at the end of the conversation?

Listening practise
This exercise should be done in threes: A, B and C.

A speaks for 2 minutes on a controversial subject which has been decided on beforehand.

B sits opposite to A and listens **without speaking.** B should convey that he or she is listening, by expression and posture, but **not** indicate any feelings about what is being said.

C is the time keeper and stops A after 2 minutes. C also notes:
- B's posture and response, and checks any speech by B
- A's manner of speech, any habits and how clearly he or she makes a point.

C does not join in the discussion.

B repeats, as clearly as possible, what A has said and A corrects any mistakes.

C comments on:
- A's habits, manner of speaking and so forth

● B's listening habits and accuracy of repetition.

At the end of the exercise, A, B and C change roles. This is done twice more so that each person has taken the role of A, B and C. When the exercise is completed, A, B and C discuss how they felt doing the exercise, and what they have learned from doing it.

Instructions should be written and handed to A, B and C before the exercise. They should be given 5 minutes to ensure that they know what they are going to do and for A to decide on the topic for discussion.

In addition to disciplining the mind to attend and concentrate on the words and behaviour of others, this exercise is designed to demonstrate that **you hear and understand much more of what others say if you cut down on your own speech.** (See notes on feedback at the end of this chapter.)

1.2 Responding

It has been said that listening is the primary skill in communicating. Responding **complements** listening.

When responding, however rushed one may be, the **impression** should be that there is **plenty of time** for the patient, client or relative. The client should feel that staff will make sure that **all** questions are answered and **all** fears are put to rest.

It is important that the client **understands** what he or she has **been told.** People in distress of any kind may need to be told something more than once, to ensure that they have really taken it in.

It is also important that the nurse or receptionist **really understands** what has been asked of him or her, and that no assumptions have been made, which may, or may not, be correct. Where there is any doubt you could say 'Can I just make sure that I have got it right? What you are asking me is . . . Is that correct?' This ensures accuracy. It also intimates to the client that what he or she says is taken seriously, and that the listener really **wants** to help.

Points to consider at the level of 'first encounters'	
	(1) The nurse manager acts as a 'buffer' between the patient or client and other people. It is his or her responsibility to ensure that they are handled sensitively and adequately.
	(2) Most of the people with whom the nurse manager will come in contact are anxious or frightened. Some are grief stricken. Occasionally they are rude, demanding, hostile or even violent.
	(3) A casual, disinterested or rude 'first encounter' may well have caused, or contributed to, inappropriate or violent behaviour. Most people are reasonable if treated with sensitivity, appropriate information given, and a reasonable and caring approach used.
	(4) It is the nurse manager's responsibility to make sure that all those within his or her span of control, who come in contact with patients, clients and relatives, are skilled in first responses.
	(5) Where exchanges can be overheard it is especially important to observe the guidelines.
	(6) Body language should reinforce what is being said and **not** be at variance with it.

The following guidelines will help when dealing with anger, hostility and violence.

Anger

Anger in the client may make you angry too! Acknowledge to yourself that this has happened but do not say 'You are making me very angry.' Try saying 'I feel angry too.' Try to determine the level of anger you feel:

'I'm annoyed' . . . 'I'm livid!'

Anger in the client should be dealt with:

- by the listener accepting that the client is angry, by saying 'I can see that you are angry', and not by belittling the anger, by saying 'I can't see why you should be angry about THAT!', or by trying to deflect it, by saying 'Shall we forget that and try to be more positive?'
- by acknowledging your own feelings, 'I feel ... concerned/frightened/bewildered'
- by clarifying what each of you wants and needs, to re-establish the relationship, 'How can we sort this out?'
- by re-establishing the relationship by considering what the experience taught each of you, and how you will deal with similar situations in the future.

Use anger as a positive force which can teach you something about yourself, and thus contribute to personal growth.

Hostility

The most important thing to remember, and possibly the most difficult thing to do, is **not to lose your temper.**

(1) Avoid the defend/attack spiral: 'It was your fault.' 'No it wasn't, it was yours.' 'Well you started it.' 'No I didn't' ... and so on. Such arguments lead to totally unproductive exchanges with no possibility of a resolution, or by a 'resolution by decibels' when the one who can shout loudest, or be most threatening, 'wins'! In fact no one wins and both feel badly.

(2) Do not interpret behaviour by saying, for example, 'You are angry because we kept you waiting.' It is one thing to **acknowledge** a person's anger by saying, 'You are angry aren't you?' It is quite another to tell someone **why** they are angry, especially as you may well be wrong!

(3) Seek information. Try to find out **why** the client is angry.

(4) Avoid using such expressions as: 'Be realistic!' 'Be fair!' 'You're not being very helpful!' 'Think how I feel!'

(5) Avoid placebos: 'Never mind! It'll soon be over.' 'Oh! Come now, it can't be **that** bad!' This is also a 'put down'.

(6) Try not to interrupt a tirade. Diffuse the situation by agreement: 'Yes, you are quite right, we really shouldn't have kept you waiting for so long. We'll try to do better next time!' 'I'm afraid I forgot to warn you that you would have a long wait. I am very sorry. Shall we start again?' It isn't easy to 'eat humble pie', but, if someone really has a legitimate grievance, it is more honest to acknowledge it, and this prevents the aggrieved person feeling that no one cares that he or she has been badly treated.

(7) In extreme cases, where everything else has failed, and you really feel that the hostility is out of proportion to the offence, conscious cold anger may be the answer: 'Mr Snooks, I have listened with patience to your complaint. I have given you my answer, and I have tried to make allowances for you, but you are disturbing others and I must now ask you to stop complaining or to leave.'

Always avoid confrontation if at all possible.

Violence

Unless you are an expert in unarmed combat, there is little you can do in the face of real violence other than to call for help, make sure you are between the violent person and the door, and get ready to run! However, there are one or two dos and don'ts which may help.

(1) Keep calm and as much in control as possible.

(2) Avoid abusive or retaliatory remarks.

(3) Do not expect the person to 'calm down' or 'keep his hair on.'

(4) Avoid smiling. Many of us, confronted by aggression, smile in an anxious kind of way. However, the client may feel that he or she is being laughed at.

(5) Try to keep the client talking. It is quite difficult to swing a punch while talking!

(6) Do not make any rash promises in the heat of the moment, which you will regret later.

(7) If you know that you will be encountering a violent patient or client, be careful not to wear a necklace, chain or necktie which could be used to choke you.

(8) If possible, get to know your patients and clients so that you can predict from your knowledge of their behaviour what incidents or problems might provoke an incident.

(9) Avoid physical contact, and try not to use physical restraint. Even if you think you are stronger and heavier than the other, remember that the adrenaline coursing through his or her veins may make that person stronger than usual!

(10) If possible, **discreetly** remove any possible weapon.

(11) Try and put some substantial object between you and the client, but don't get trapped behind a desk or in a corner.

(12) If you find yourself losing your temper, get out, **fast**!

(13) Following the incident ensure that you review what happened so that you can avoid similar encounters in the future.

(14) Warn colleagues of potential, future problems from that quarter.

1.3 Asking questions

Questioning at the primary level will be mainly concerned with acquiring information. **Closed** and **open** questions will be employed for this purpose.

Closed questions

These are questions which elicit single-word answers. They are very useful to establish facts but will not progress a conversation that seeks to explore feelings, thoughts or attitudes. For example, 'Do you wish to see me?' They can also be used to obtain information that has only a factual content. For example, 'What is your surname?' **Never** ask 'What is your Christian name'?

Open questions

These allow the respondent to express his or her thoughts and they help the questioner to learn more about the needs, attitudes and concerns of another. For example, 'How can I help you?'

Exercise 6

Over the next week note the responses you get to closed questions. Were you forced to ask **another question** to get the information you sought?

1.4 Giving instructions or information

The first person to contact clients, patients or relatives is frequently in the position of being asked for information. For example, 'How long will I have to wait for the results?' 'Who will look after my cat while I am in hospital?' 'Will the District Nurse come to visit me every day?'

Information given via the telephone

It has been shown that **good** communication entails the use of all senses to try to make sense of the signals people send to each other. The impossibility of seeing the communicator, while using the telephone, eliminates all the senses except that of hearing. Thus the only clues to the reactions of the person at the other end of the telephone are the use of language and the inflections of the voice. In such circumstances the skills of careful, accurate listening are even more important.

Telephone operators are busy and often hard-pressed people. Occasionally they answer so quickly that the beginning of an announcement is lost. For example, the operator might have **said** 'St Angela's Hospital' but the listener only **heard** '. . . pital'. In such a case the listener does **not** know if he or she has got through to the right number.

When next you telephone your place of work note:

(1) Whether the person answering makes it clear that you are through to the number you wanted.
(2) How accurately, sympathetically and quickly your question, or request, is responded to.
(3) How well your message is dealt with.

Instructing learners in simple techniques

The stages of such instruction and its consequent learning are:

● explanation of the process, its purpose and why and when it is used
● demonstration of the process, or part of the process
● practise by the learner
● positive reinforcement by the teacher, for example, 'You did that very well' or 'You've almost got it, try once more'
● continued practise until the learner is proficient.

Errors that teachers make are:

(1) Expecting the learner to assimilate a number of processes or a long or involved process at one time. Break up a task into small elements and go through all the stages of learning for each one, making sure that each has been learned before progressing to the next. **Build** on each stage.

(2) Expecting involved processes to be learned too quickly by failing to recognise:
   (a) that **your familiarity** with the process may make you underestimate its difficulty
   (b) that everyone learns at a different pace and that the 'slow' learner may not be stupid − the learner's failure to learn may be your failure to communicate effectively. **Review your technique.**
   (c) that people learn in different ways. To some a demonstration and a verbal description of what is happening may be most effective. Others may prefer to take written instructions and puzzle them out alone. Some people do not like to admit that they have not understood, particularly if you have made it clear that you do not 'suffer fools gladly'. Visual aids and humour are of great value.

Do not use jargon which the learner cannot understand.

2. Qualities needed in primary communications

2.1 Desire to help

It is often the case that the feeling 'I have had it up to here with everyone wanting something' can be communicated verbally to the next person who comes along by 'I haven't got ten pairs of hands.'

2.2 Patience

Patience is particularly important with the elderly, whose thought processes may be slower than yours, and with those dazed with pain or grief. Unfortunately it is not always possible to judge who is suffering in this way, and people with great worries or under great stress can be given quite insensitive treatment.

2.3 Respect for others

Every human being is unique. Rejoicing in this quality of uniqueness means that you may **not agree** with another's morals, attitudes or beliefs, but you recognise that individual's right to hold them. It is your right to feed back to others how their behaviour affects you, but it is ultimately up to them to decide whether or not they will change it. This is the quality of empathy.

2.4 Sincerity

It is possible to assume an appearance of interest, patience or respect without feeling these qualities; it is rarely that this will not be recognised.

The question 'Who cares for the carers?' has often been asked. The answer should be **their managers.** Sincerity in caring for people will mean sensitivity for those with a stressful and often thankless job. The nurse manager has in his or her care, not only patients, clients and relatives, but learners, often young and vulnerable, and colleagues who depend on their friends to help when life gets too difficult.

For discussion

Sitting in a restaurant waiting to be served, a man observed that the people at the next table were rude to the waiter and left without giving him a tip. The waiter banged the dishes together, muttering under his breath, then turned to the man and thrust the menu at him with a furious look.

The man said: 'I can see that you are angry because of the behaviour of those customers, but it's not **my** fault they behaved badly! Think of it this way. If you allow yourself to take it out on me, **I** won't leave a tip either, so **you** will be the loser!'

2.5 Respecting confidentiality and privacy

Health care workers are usually well aware of the necessity to respect information given to them in confidence. In OPD, accident and emergency departments or where appointments are made, confidentiality is often difficult, because of the proximity of other patients. Doctors, examining patients, may only be separated from the next patient by a curtain, and intimate details can be overheard. Every effort should be made to avoid this and to avoid leaving patients' notes in places accessible to those who should not see them. Take the time to look at your area of work and check how well the patients' privacy is respected. What measures are taken to ensure confidentiality?

2.6 Dependability

Information given must **always** be accurate. A patient, helpful approach must **always** be shown. Respect for others must **always** be shown.

2.7 Ability to put others at ease

Are you the kind of person others **want** to talk to?

Exercise 8

Use a tape recorder to record how you deal with people at first encounters. If you get someone else to work the equipment, you will soon forget it is there. Your natural approach to others will then reveal itself! Did you sound: Cold? Impatient? Patronising? Bad tempered? Sarcastic? Warm? Patient? Helpful? Re-assuring?

Secondary communications

Unlike primary communications, secondary communications indicate on-going inter-personal relationships. The nurse manager will use such communications with patients, clients and their families; with professional colleagues in his or her peer group, as well as with other professionals; and with those he or she manages.

1. Skills and knowledge needed in secondary communications

All the skills, knowledge and qualities used in primary communications are necessary for companionable, capable and efficient inter-personal relationships. In addition there are other useful skills which can be improved or developed.

1.1 Paraphrasing

It has already been shown that in lengthy communications the listener's concentration can be lost. How can the listener maintain his or her concentration and, at the same time, check on how accurately he or she has heard what was said? It helps, in this context, to stop a speaker (preferably when he or she pauses for breath!) by saying 'May I stop you there for a moment? What I hear you saying is that you were reluctant to marry your present husband but, because of pressure from your parents, you did so. You soon found that you had little in common and that from time to time he was liable to become violent. You began to drink heavily last year and you are now worried about this and about how to get out of the whole situation. Have I got it right so far?' This reinforces the messages in **your mind** and demonstrates the fact that you are really attending to what is being said. It also helps the speaker to 'hear him or herself' and clarify his or her thoughts.

1.2 Flagging

Out of the mishmash of thoughts and ideas presented it may be desirable to recall or 'flag' one or two of the themes which need to be followed up. For example, during the paraphrase, you might 'flag', as of vital importance to the story:

- the reluctant marriage
- the violence
- the heavy drinking
- the desire to change the situation.

You might then ask the client to choose **one** of these topics to pursue in greater detail.

1.3 Using silence

In every day conversations silences can be uncomfortable, but they are often an indication that the listener is gathering his or her ideas in readiness to progress to the next sequence of thoughts. In such cases, the temptation is to 'jump in' with some thoughts of one's own. However, if one has enough patience and strength of will, keeping silent will often encourage the speaker to continue to speak.

There is, of course, a point at which a silence becomes too protracted and uncomfortable, and the speaker can then become tense or distrustful. The skill is to gauge how long one can maintain a silence **profitably.** When a silence becomes unbearable try repeating, in question form, the client's last sentence. For example, 'I found him very difficult to live with' 'You found him difficult to live with?' 'Yes, he was . . .'

Exercise 9

The next time you have a conversation with someone who is disclosing personal information to you, try to maintain silence. **See how much more the other person will contribute.**

1.4 Negotiating

Much of our communication with others is aimed at getting them to do something. There are a number of ways in which the nurse manager can do this:

- by issuing an order
- by making a request
- by negotiating an action.

Negotiating indicates a discussion between two or more people whereby both **understand** what is required of them and **agree** to carry it out. Successful negotiating leaves both parties satisfied that they have gained something. Neither may have achieved **all** that is wanted, but both feel reasonably happy with the agreement arrived at.

There are times to issue orders and times to negotiate an agreement. Obviously when work is going on in a ward, for example, it would not be sensible to enter into negotiations as to what someone is to do as a matter of urgency. Changes in **policy** or **routine procedures** will be brought about much more smoothly if both the manager and the staff:

- understand **clearly** what is to happen
- have had an opportunity to discuss the changes and express how they feel about them
- if necessary, make small adjustments to the changes, rather than **basic** alterations. This will satisfy **both** of you that the changes can be beneficial and painless!

In negotiating **avoid:**

- taking up a hard and fast position
- having a blazing row
- going into the defend/attack spiral, which is a mode of discussion whereby each person defends his or her own point of view and refuses to recognise any quality of argument in what the other has to say. It is an unprofitable way of communicating as neither person is prepared to give way and no negotiating can take place.

To negotiate successfully **negotiate an improvement.** Nurses, being in the habit of taking orders, often:

- accept without question any instructions from senior management, or
- accept the orders but complain to each other without doing anything to try to change them.

A more productive way of behaving would be to:

- say 'I will look at it and let you know' or 'May I have some time to think about this?'
- consider the proposals carefully and, if they seem rational, accept them
- think out how they might be improved, if they are not acceptable
- **negotiate** the improvements.

If you have negotiated successfully **at the end of the discussions the relationship should be improved** (Figure 6).

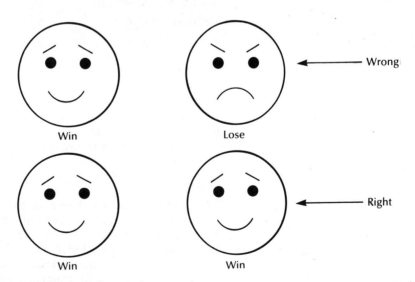

Figure 6   The effects of negotiating

It has been shown that negotiating is an important aspect of management. The manager who has harmonious relationships within his or her area of work is the one who:

- knows when to issue an order and when to consult and negotiate
- has the trust of his or her staff so that they will know that his or her management style is not normally autocratic and that they can depend on him or her to consult them where this is preferable.

Assertive rights	As human beings living in a democratic society we all have basic assertive rights.

(1) **The right to express thoughts and feelings.** We all have a right to say, for example, 'I don't like that' or 'I feel very angry at having to change duty without warning. It interferes with my personal life.'

(2) **The right to have these thoughts and feelings respected.** Expressing what you object to and having your objections respected means that others recognise your feelings and understand your point of view. It is useless complaining to others without telling your boss. Moreover it is disruptive and dishonest. Expressing your feelings **in a calm and reasonable manner is the best way to have your rights respected.**

(3) **The right to be listened to and taken seriously.**

(4) **The right to ask for what you want.**

(5) **The right to make mistakes!** Everyone does at times!

(6) **The right to ask for information. Choose your time.** It really can be irritating if people ask for information at the wrong time. Remember your boss has rights too.

(7) **The right to say 'no'.** You have the right to say 'No I will not work late tonight.' Before you do so, however, weigh up what will happen as a result of your refusal. You might be better saying 'I do not wish to work late tonight but, if you have tried every other possibility and can assure me that there is no other option, I will consider it again.'

(8) **The right to make a decision on one's own terms.** 'I do not wish to take part in the evening meetings which you are proposing.'

(9) **The right not to feel guilty.** You should never be put in the position of feeling badly about any decision you have made. If you do you should express this feeling to your boss.

(10) **The right to choose not to be assertive.** You have the right not to 'speak up for yourself' if you do not wish to do so.

2. Qualities needed in secondary communications

2.1 Leadership

As the leader of a team a nurse manager is responsible for the following:

Leading and directing

The nurse manager:

- says how and when things will be done and evaluates and monitors how well they have been done
- says what is to be done and sets standards as to the quality and quantity of the work
- provides information to the workforce regarding the policies of the organisation and any instructions which are issued on its behalf
- is responsible for the achievement of the goals of the organisation and ensures that, in his or her sphere of influence, they are carried out.

Coaching staff

The use of the word 'coach' may be somewhat confusing but it indicates the fact that the nurse manager not only **tells** staff what is required by the organisation or by him or her in efforts to maintain standards, but also **explains** to staff why these things are required and why policies are necessary. The nurse manager also ensures that staff **understand** what the standards of the organisation are and why it is essential to maintain them.

Acting as a facilitator to the staff

The facilitating faculty of a nurse manager is aimed at ensuring that every aspect of the work of the staff is made as easy as possible by being there to offer support, to help in problem solving, to co-ordinate group activities and to make sure that, within the group, relationships are harmonious, strong and cohesive. The nurse manager will also 'protect' staff from outside pressures, taking these pressures upon him or herself, and only sharing them if there is a need to improve or change the work the subordinates have to do.

Delegating responsibility and accountability to subordinates

Delegation means having the trust and confidence in staff to allow them to get on with the delegated work without constant, and possibly irritating, supervision. It also means **giving praise for a job well done.**

More will be said about leadership and leadership styles in another book in this series, *Managing Others*.

2.2 Empathy

This indicates a non-judgemental attitude towards a client which leaves the client free to examine his or her behaviour and its effect on others, and, through feedback, to determine whether he or she should seek to change it.

2.3 Feedback

Joe Luft[1] and Harry Ingham proposed the idea that, in a relationship between two people, four areas of the 'self' affect the communication. They described this by using a model which they called the Johari Window. The areas described were:

(1) What a person knows about him or herself and is prepared to share with others — the 'public self'.
(2) What a person knows about him or herself but is inclined not to disclose — the 'private self'. This includes fears, doubts, anxieties, fantasies, feelings of conflict and confusion, dreams and ambitions which are fragile and easily destroyed..
(3) What others may know about a person but which that person may not know personally — the 'bad breath' area, the area of personal habits or attitudes.
(4) What is unknown, at least consciously, to a person or to others — the 'unknown'.

The Johari Window as described diagrammatically is shown in Figure 7.

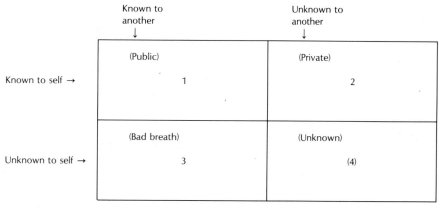

Figure 7   The Johari Window

The objective should be to expand areas 1 and 3 and to contract areas 2 and 4. This would help a person to know more about him or herself so that he or she could change any unacceptable behaviour and share more of him or herself with others. This can be best achieved by counselling or by feedback. Feedback, given by another, helps a person gain insight into how his or her behaviour affects others and reveals things about the person which he or she may be unaware.

Rules for feedback

There are, however, a number of 'rules' concerned with feedback which must be observed if it is to be of value:

(1) Do **not** seek feedback from others if you are not prepared to **accept** or, at least, **consider** it. To expand the boundaries requires trust in the giver of feedback and involves a certain amount of risk taking in the recipient.

(2) Feedback is most effective when **asked for,** as opposed to that which is unsolicited. Assertive behaviour, however, may demand that you offer feedback without it being demanded. **How** it is given is vital. For example, do **not** say 'You are very rude.' Try saying 'When you speak to me like that you make me feel very angry and anxious.'

(3) It should be given as soon as possible following the observed behaviour.

(4) It is very effective when given during group work, as you can check with others in the group that your perceptions of the behaviour are in accord with theirs.

(5) It must be **descriptive** of **your reaction** to the behaviour and **not** seek to evaluate it. For example, do **not** say 'You are a very nice person.' Try saying 'I like you very much.'

(6) It should be **specific** rather than **general** in describing behaviour. For example, do **not** say 'You are a very opinionated person.' Try saying 'When you were speaking just now I felt that I must accept your opinion or risk a "put down" if I offered a different one.'

(7) Never offer feedback on behaviour which another cannot change.

(8) If **you** receive feedback, it may be helpful to check, with the giver and with other group members, that you are correct in what you believe was intended.

In a group, members will often rush to the defence of someone who they think is being 'attacked'. You may not have **intended** an attack but if that is how it appeared to others it is wise to ask yourself:

- Was the feedback given aggressively?
- Was it evaluative in nature?
- Was it inappropriate in any other way?

When asked to comment on how another person performed while doing an exercise or a role play, there is often a reluctance to do so. Comments such as 'Well I think she was very good' may be meant to re-assure and help, but they are seldom constructive. It is important that, when asked to offer **constructive feedback,** members are helped:

- to offer feedback sensitively
- to understand that only by being given accurate feedback can others learn about themselves. This may entail commenting on the negative aspects of the behaviour observed as well as the positive aspects.

References

1. Joseph Luft, *Group Processes: An Introduction to Group Dynamics* (National Press Books, 1963, 1970).

Suggested further reading

Ken Back and Kate Back, *Assertiveness at Work* (London: McGraw-Hill, 1982).

Pamela E. Butler, *Self-assertion for Women* (New York: Harper & Row, 1981).

Roger Fisher and William Ury, *Getting to Yes: Negotiating Agreement without Giving In* (Hutchinson, 1982, 1986).

Gavin Kennedy, *Everything is Negotiable* (Business Books Ltd., 1982, 1983).

Joseph Luft, *Of Human Interaction: The Johari Model* (Mayfield Publishing Company, 1969).

Sheila Marson, ed., *Managing Others* (Macmillan Education, 1990).

Chapter 3

The communications continuum: coaching and counselling

Advice giving – information giving

There are three aspects of 'advice giving' for which the nurse manager is responsible in his or her day-to-day work:

(1) Teaching/coaching staff.
(2) Educating staff and the public.
(3) Informing staff, peers, patients, clients and relatives.

1. Teaching/coaching

Management coaching, in its interpretive sense, has already been discussed. Interpreting the needs and policies of the organisation is, however, only one aspect of the coaching role of the nurse manager. The second responsibility of the nurse manager in this area is to ensure the development of staff, the human resource of the organisation, and to make the organisation aware of the human assets it controls. This involves continuous on-the-job training and, although time consuming, is vital for the maintenance of an able workforce.

Collectively, nurse managers are responsible for the maintenance of nursing standards; for the well being of the general public in the area of health care and, in co-operation with other health care workers, for the quality and cost effectiveness of the service provided.

A number of factors contribute to the maintenance of such a workforce.

1.1 Role modelling

Those new to a profession, seeking their own professional identity and management style, will often model themselves on an established member of the profession who they admire and who appears to them to be successful. This places considerable responsibility on nurse managers to demonstrate good practice at all times, so that the role modelled is acceptable and appropriate. Many nurses have a tower of influence on their juniors of which they may be unaware.

1.2 Assessments and appraisal

In the course of his or her work the nurse manager will be continually assessing the team members with the objectives of helping them:

- to recognise their strengths and weaknesses
- to build on their strengths and to correct their weaknesses
- to recognise and develop their potential in present and future roles.

The ultimate aim of continuous assessment leads to appraisal with its setting of, and management by, objectives. It should be noted here that appraisal is more accurately described as **staff development** and **performance review** (SD & PR) as its aim is the personal and career development of staff (see Chapter 5).

1.3 Training

To help in the development of the team member, the nurse manager must be aware of training which is appropriate and available to the team. The nurse manager should, therefore, be in close contact with:

- regional and district training or personnel departments
- nurse training departments.

27

If information is not readily available, it may be necessary for the nurse manager to contact these departments personally. If communications in the unit are working well, however, the nurse manager should, as a matter of course, have access to such information. It is wise for the nurse manager to establish and maintain a good relationship with training departments and to check, at regular intervals, what is on offer. In addition the nurse manager should make sure that he or she is aware of national training, conferences, workshops and seminars, and of training arranged by the professional bodies.

2. Educating

While teaching/coaching is usually confined to professional matters, education, in its broadest sense, as a lifelong progression and process, is something that is basically the responsibility of the individual.

The responsibility of the nurse manager in this area is to facilitate and encourage by advice, and to provide as much information and practical help as possible. The nurse manager can suggest areas of further study, which may be of particular value to the team member whose strengths and weaknesses the nurse manager knows well.

The education of the general public, particularly for community staff, is also an area in which the nurse manager will be involved. Making public presentations is always difficult, particularly when training in this skill has not been received. A chapter on making presentations is included in this book. It might be useful for the nurse manager who may be involved in work of this kind to attend some training events which would help in overcoming nervousness, and which would suggest better and more effective ways of making presentations.

3. Information giving

The skills of information giving are:

- All those discussed in primary and secondary communications.
- Knowledge of the subject, particularly on the rare occasions when advice is offered.
- Knowledge of when to refer an enquirer, and who or where to refer them to.
- Teaching skills.
- Presentational skills.

3.1 To staff and/or peers

This type of information is usually related to professional matters or may be obtained in the course of sharing information or teaching.

3.2 To patients and/or clients

This is an area where the nurse manager needs to be very clear of his or her responsibility and to the pitfalls inherent when 'giving information' becomes 'giving advice'. It has been argued that no one can advise another person for three very viable reasons:

(1) Not knowing what may be the questions behind the request for advice, or the problems which the seeker of advice suffers. In such a situation, it is not possible to offer the kind of advice which will be **wise** and **appropriate.**
(2) By offering advice, a person may be impeding the development of the problem-solving abilities of the advice seeker.
(3) By offering **unsolicited** advice, the offerer insults the intelligence of the recipient by implying that that person is incapable of solving his or her own problems.

There are times when 'advice' must be offered, but even then it should be recognised that ultimate **decisions** belong to the individual.

Rules for giving advice	(1) Avoid giving advice as much as possible.
	(2) Give as much **information** as possible, and be quite sure that it is accurate.
	(3) Lay out, before the advice seeker, all the options and all the actions that might be taken.

Exercise 10

A woman who had a child with a genetic defect asked 'Does this mean that I should not have any more children?' How would you answer?

It might be most helpful to say something like 'Let me put it this way. It is a proven fact that women who have had one child with this defect run a 20% (or 40% or 100%) risk that all subsequent children will have the same defect.'

The **facts** are now before the woman. **She** must decide what to do about them.

There are occasionally those for whom decisions must be made, however, and there may be occasions when it will be necessary to say 'I therefore strongly advise you to . . .' Can you think of any such occasions?

Primary counselling

Figure 5 shows that primary counselling consists of two main elements:

(1) Dealing with problems and anxieties (helping and befriending).
(2) Counselling at work.

It is, however, necessary to try and understand what is meant by 'counselling', particularly as the term is frequently used in an imprecise manner. This can perhaps be best done by considering what factors have been identified as contributing to the definition of the word and describe the boundaries of the task.

1. Activities of counselling

- Counselling is a **professional relationship** between a trained, competent counsellor and a client who needs help to alter, modify or change his or her behaviour. Rogers[1] calls it 'the process by which the structure of the self is relaxed in the safety of the relationship with the therapist, and previously denied experiences are perceived and then integrated into an altered self.'

- Counselling is a **process concerned with decision making and problem solving**. The counsellor, having formed a relationship with the client, helps the client to define the problem(s) in his or her life and gives the client the space to seek for solutions.

- Counselling is an **education for life**. Learning the skills of problem solving gives the client an expanded range of abilities, which can be used in situations outside the immediate counselling environment.

- Counselling is an **enabling process** in the learning of new behaviour or attitudes. The client learns about his or her life-space and recognises how his or her attitudes and behaviour affect others. By gaining an understanding of him or herself, the client is helped to take positive action to improve relationships. Only by the positive demonstration of changed behaviour on the part of the client can the counsellor judge the effectiveness of their work together.

- Counselling is a **collaborative enterprise** entered into by two people, with its progress marked by the setting and attaining of goals and contracts.

- Counselling is a **cluster of skills** which can be used in many forms of communication, but which, when used in a deliberate and sequential way, lead the client through a number of stages to the resolution of a problem.

- Counselling is a **way of life**. Once a counsellor learns the more effective ways of behaving towards others to facilitate relationships, he or she cannot then behave in another way. The counselling skills acquired are not reserved for specific times or places, but are constant in all relationships.

- Counselling is a **positive activity**. Counselling should help the client. At the very least, it never damages the client. In Carl Rogers's terms, it is **client centred and non-judgemental.**

By looking at each of these eight activities, you can perhaps decide whether you can claim to **offer** counselling or whether you are **using** counselling skills, and thereby communicating effectively and helpfully.

2. Dealing with problems and anxieties

Even when a nurse manager is a trained and competent counsellor, there are other factors that influence the decision to enter into a counselling relationship with a patient or client.

2.1 Time

The counselling process, while not completely open ended, does entail offering the patient or client a reasonably elastic period of time, or a number of sessions with defined limits, within which to resolve the problems together. This immediately precludes many individuals who, in a busy life, cannot take on such a commitment.

2.2 Role

Neither the nurse manager nor the organisation employing the nurse manager may define counselling as part of the manager's role and the nurse manager will, in these circumstances, prefer to refer those who seek counselling to an 'outside' counsellor. In the case of health care staff, this help will probably be found in the Occupational Health Centre.

2.3 Appropriateness

In addition to patients and/or clients, counselling may be sought by members of the nurse manager's team. This raises questions of an ethical and practical nature. These are discussed in the next section. In the light of these questions, the nurse manager may decide that personal counselling would not be appropriate.

3. Counselling at work

Managers have a clearly defined role within an organisation. It expects them to maintain a workforce which is hardworking and productive, and which will accurately interpret and carry out company policy. If the workforce is contented, it is more likely to attain these objectives, so managers are expected, within reasonable limits, to ensure that the physical, mental and intellectual needs of the workforce are cared for.

For the purpose of this discussion, the NHS is described as a 'Company', and companies who employ and pay their managers expect loyalty and competence. A company cannot be a therapeutic institution, but, within the limits of its cost-effective environment, it wishes to maintain good relationships with its workforce, and to be seen as a good employer.

The foregoing comments apply in every organisation, irrespective of whether it manufactures nuts and bolts or delivers health care. How the manager sees the workforce will affect the way in which individuals are treated. The manager alone is accountable for those who work under his or her command and, when a subordinate approaches a manager for help or counselling, caused by some life crisis, the manager is the mediator and exponent of the ethos of the organisation.

Whatever the problem, the nurse manager may be asked, in the future, to write a reference for a subordinate, or at least to make some assessment. The nurse manager may also be asked to offer an opinion as to the subordinate's fitness for promotion. However caring the manager may be, circumstances in the subordinate's past will inevitably be remembered and influence the manager's response. Moreover the manager must remember that it would be a failure of duty to the company to ignore such matters, or cover up anything that could affect the subordinate's future competence.

One way out of this dilemma is to refer those with such problems to the Occupational Health Service, if it exists. This service has a sophisticated role since it exists within the territory of the health authority, but maintains its professional independence and confidentiality. Only when health centre staff are acting as agents of the organisation – for example, at pre-employment screening – may a report be made to the prospective employer, and even then such a report would be with the consent of the prospective employee. The only other occasion on which information could be divulged would be that in which the employee's 'problem' might make him or her a danger to him or herself or others. Again the employee would be warned that this information would need to be passed to management.

The most honest way of dealing with these problems is to ensure that, at the outset, the worker is made aware of the manager's responsibility to the organisation and the ways in which help can be obtained, and to help by support and encouragement.

Rules for counselling	(1) There may be some nurse managers who are **specifically appointed** to undertake counselling.
	(2) The majority of nurse managers do not have counselling as a remit in their role specification.
	(3) All nurse managers should use counselling skills when helping and befriending patients, relatives or clients.
	(4) Counselling subordinates is unwise. However, it is essential to be aware of places where they can go for help.

3.1 Career counselling

The first step in career counselling is management coaching, when the organisation and its policies are interpreted to members of the team. The second focal point of career counselling is associated with assessments and SD & PR.

This will be discussed at greater length in another section, and you can read more in Chapter 8 of *Managing Yourself*, another volume in this series.[2]

4. Skills of primary counselling

(1) All those discussed in primary and secondary communications (see Chapter 2).
(2) An ability to assess subordinates **impartially** and a willingness to help them.
(3) Knowledge of when help is appropriate and when it is not, and of who can offer this help.
(4) An ability to help in bringing about change. This encompasses:
    (a) institutional change (to be dealt with in a following book in this series)
    (b) personal change, which indicates self-knowledge, a wish to change, and the willingness and wisdom of team members to help.

Secondary counselling

This area has two branches.

1. Therapeutic counselling

A discussion of therapeutic counselling is beyond the scope of this book. Few nurse managers are involved in therapeutic counselling and a wide range of literature exists for those who are involved. Little needs to be said, therefore, except to point out that this is an area in which the untrained have no place.

2. Co-counselling and support groups

2.1 Co-counselling

This is also a very specific 'skill area' and numerous courses and workshops can be found which offer training in this field. It is meant to provide mutual support for trained counsellors involved in counselling, and involves a considerable amount of their time.

2.2 Support groups

These are of great value for **all** health care workers. The tendency to argue that staff in some work areas are subjected to greater stress than in others can be questioned. Stress, and reactions to it, are very individual matters and it might be more profitable to accept that all those caring for the sick, disabled, old or relatives need to be given support. This should take the form of offering them the opportunity to off-load their anxieties and to seek the comfort and re-assurance of colleagues, psychologists and counsellors who are experienced in running support groups.

Some areas of the Health Service are already establishing support groups, and they are proving invaluable in preventing illness and absenteeism, and in avoiding 'burn out', which can create apparently uncaring bored staff or lead to staff leaving the profession.

2.3 Multi-disciplinary support groups

These groups, led by an experienced group leader, are especially useful as they have the added advantage of helping different sections of staff to understand each other's problems, and thus to become more co-operative, patient and understanding in their reactions to one another.

Exercise 11

Sue is frequently late and her nurse manager delays commenting on this until it becomes so consistent that she can no longer ignore it. One morning she calls Sue into her office and the following dialogue takes place:

Miss Smith: Sue, I am very concerned that you are consistently late these days. As you live relatively nearby I cannot understand why this is so.

Sue: It's the buses Miss Smith. They're so unreliable!

Miss Smith: Yes, but you will just have to get up half an hour earlier won't you? Besides it's not only that you're always late. When you get here you walk about in a dream! You really will have to pull your socks up if you expect me to give you a good report! Now, go and get on with your work and **no more lateness!**

Sue: Yes, but . . .

Miss Smith: No Sue, I don't want excuses. It's up to you to do better. If you are late again I will have to take other measures. Go along now and get on with your work.

Exit Sue – not far from tears.

(1) What happened in this exchange?
(2) How do you think Sue felt?
(3) What could have been behind Sue's lateness and tiredness?
(4) How might Miss Smith have helped her?

Later in the morning in the staff room Miss Smith could have been heard saying to a colleague: 'I had to have Sue White in for counselling this morning. She's **always** late and she wanders about half asleep when she does manage to get in!'

(5) How would **you** describe the interview? Was it:
    (a) a counselling interview?
    (b) a disciplinary interview?

---

3. Discipline

Discipline is necessary, but it is wise to consider these points:

● Always tell someone they have done something wrong the **first** time it happens. Do not wait until it has become a problem.
● Give the other person the opportunity to offer an explanation, and try to find an answer to the problem together.
● Always be aware of the possibility of an underlying problem which could explain the inadequate behaviour. If necessary, refer the person concerned to someone who can help.
● **Never** confuse a **disciplinary interview** with a **counselling interview.**

References

1. Carl R. Rogers, *Client-centered Therapy* (Constable, 1981).
2. Verena Tschudin and Jane Schober, *Managing Yourself* (London: Macmillan, 1990).

Suggested further reading

Tanya Arroba and Kim James, *Pressure at Work: A Survival Guide* (McGraw-Hill, 1987).

Gerard Egan, *The Skilled Helper* (Brooks/Cole Publishing Co., 1980).

Richard Nelson-Jones, *Human Relationship Skills: Training and Self-help* (Cassell, 1986).

Michael Reddy, *The Manager's Guide to Counselling at Work* (The British Psychological Society and Methuen, 1987).

Part II Using Communications in Management

Part II of this book looks at ways, other than those already described, in which communications influence management tasks.

Chapter 4   Planning and organising

Introduction

The functions of management are usually described as:

- planning
- organising
- staffing
- leading
- controlling
- co-ordinating.

This chapter discusses the first two functions, planning and organising. Chapter 5 is devoted to staffing issues while Chapter 6 considers co-ordination skills. The subjects of leading and controlling are discussed in other books in the series, *Managing Others* and *Managing Change*, and readers are referred to these.

Planning

1. Decision making and problem solving

Constant decision making is a feature of everyday life and most of our decisions are based on custom and habit. For example, it is usual to dress before going into the world outside the home, the principal decision-making process being associated with the choice of the kind of dress to be worn. This choice may require marshalling a number of facts. Is it Summer or Winter? Is it cold or warm? Who will I meet? What will I be doing? What impression do I wish to make? The human brain is well adapted to making such choices with a minimum of effort even though, of itself, each choice may be a fairly sophisticated one.

Decisions taken at work are usually of a different nature, affecting personal development, the effectiveness of the team, organisation or profession, and frequently having wide implications for a number of people. Research by NASA, the American Space Agency, has revealed that decisions made by teams are usually more effective than those taken by individuals.

Brainstorming

This is a method of team decision making. The only requirement is a black or white board or a 'flip' chart. The problem is described and team members are asked to call out any solutions which they can think of. However unlikely the solutions appear, they are **all** written down on the board or flip chart. When all possible solutions have been offered and written down, each is discussed, to consider:

- which are obviously untenable
- which are possible but not likely to be very effective
- which are most useful.

The untenable suggestions are put to one side and the remaining suggestions are graded on an ascending scale of feasibility. The most appropriate solution is chosen and tested. If it works, there is no need to return to the other solutions. If the chosen solution does **not** work, the next solution can be tried, and so on.

The solution of problems should be a systematic exercise, and if the following steps are taken, no stage will be forgotten (see Figure 8):

(1) Define the problem – this may require considerable discussion remembering that, as in medicine, the **symptoms are not the disease.**
(2) Consider the solutions – brainstorming.

(3) Choose a solution.
(4) Implement the solution.
(5) Evaluate its effect.
(6) If the problem is 'cured', no further action is necessary. If it is not, return to (1), as the reason for the failure may be that the **real problem** was not identified.

Figure 8 A problem-solving model

Decision making and problem solving are crucial to effective management at all levels. In the words of Drucker[1] 'Whatever a manager does, he does through making decisions.' However, despite their importance, the majority of managers tend to solve problems and make decisions with little heed for any systematic process. Like dressing before going out, many decisions are made because habit dictates not only that they **should** be made, but often that they are made in a manner decided by custom. Such routine decisions are relatively easy to arrive at but, from time to time, managers must make decisions on questions or procedures unfamiliar to them. The manager must then produce an answer which will not only be objective, but will have an above average chance of being effective in its aims and will be acceptable to those who it will affect. To achieve this, a systemic approach **must** be employed.

Strategic decisions, which involve making changes or using resources in a more effective way, should never be arrived at through problem solving. This does not mean that such decisions are not capable of being made through systematic operations. In fact, the decision-making process can follow similar lines to the problem-solving process already described:

(1) Define the decision to be made.
(2) Analyse the decision by asking:
    (a) Why do you want to change this/these things?
    (b) What decision is asked for?
    (c) What will it change?
    (d) What will it achieve?
    (e) Who will it effect?
    (f) How will it effect them?
    (g) Is the result likely to be worth the 'upset' of making the change?
(3) What alternatives are there?
(4) Choose the 'best' alternative (keeping the others in reserve).

(5) Implement and evaluate it.
(6) Return to (1) if the chosen alternative is not successful.

One of the arguments against using such techniques is that they are too time consuming, and time is the one thing most busy nurse managers have little of. Note that 'bad' decisions, arrived at without careful consideration, are much more time consuming and can be damaging in other ways.

Exercise 12

Your manager has told you that, because of cost, you may have to lose two of your staff.

(1) When you have considered the problem carefully, what further information would you seek?
(2) **On your own,** think out and make a list of the ways in which you might achieve the proposed cuts. Place these in order of acceptability.
(3) **In a group,** work through the problem-solving process (see Figure 8).
(4) Compare (2) and (3). Were the decisions similar or different? If they were different, in what way was this so?

---

2. Developing strategies and policies

Strategic decisions can be locally conceived and developed, or be part of the organisational framework. In both cases, however, as things change at the local or organisational level, so the original strategy **must** also develop if the organisation is to avoid becoming a monolithic institution. Such dynamic development will depend on:

- Experience, carefully analysed to ensure that it is acting as a catalyst, rather than being an automatic response to provide an answer.
- Experimentation.
- Research. Nurse managers will wish to know if new strategies and policies are working, need updating or would benefit from minor changes.

Research does not have to be an esoteric exercise carried out by special researchers. Many simple data-gathering exercises can, and should, be under-taken as part of the manager's daily work. Not only should statistical data be gathered, but also opinions. If, for example, a change affects clients or patients, why not **ask them** how they feel about it? Industrialists are constantly carrying out market research, yet, all too often in the NHS, the tendency seems to be to wait for complaints!

Collecting statistical and opinion-generated data is not only valuable to show the way in which strategies and policies can be developed, but also provides a tool for the manager who has to make a case for improved resources.

3. Implementing strategies and policies

The necessity to involve members of a team in decision making and problem solving has already been stressed. The implementation of these strategies and policies also needs a team decision to resolve such questions as:

- When shall we start?
- Where or with whom?
- Who will do it and how?
- For how long?
- How will we know if it works?
- What data shall we collect?
- When shall we meet again to review progress?

Organising

1. Team building

It is now some years since the concept of the boss as the head of the enterprise began to change, and that of team management began to take its place. Since that time most firms, from small to large, and almost all institutions have adopted the new concept. On practical, moral and ethical grounds this concept seemed to be more acceptable, ensuring the participation and commitment of all professions and disciplines, and preventing the wielding of supreme power by one person.

The need for one person to be ultimately responsible and accountable will remain, but, by involving others – the team – in decision making and problem solving, his or her management can only be improved.

Questions soon arose as to what made a 'good' team and how such a team could be assembled. Two very prestigious institutions, The Administrative Staff College at Henley and The Industrial Training Research Unit at Cambridge, collaborated to set up experimental teams and to judge their effectiveness, demonstrated through management games and later by the establishment of teams in industrial settings. Belbin[2] described the process and the results, and delineated the successful and unsuccessful teams. Sophisticated personality and intelligence tests were used in the experiments to identify 'types' whose attributes would combine to produce successful teams.

It is unlikely that such techniques would be used at the first-line nurse manager level to assemble teams, since, at this level of management, team members are rarely appointed by their immediate team leader or manager. However, a number of facts emerged from the research which are of interest and importance to all managers at every level, and when applied to management teams can improve performance:

- When asked to make a 'good' manager appointment, panels are usually looking for the good all-rounder. They are also looking for the most intelligent of the applicants, and are rarely prepared to appoint those who have had their weaknesses exposed either at the interview or through references. The Henley–Cambridge experience showed that every team member would have **allowable weaknesses,** which would be compensated by personal strengths or by the strengths of other team members.
- Each member of the ideal team was seen as taking a specific role in its composition (see Table 3).
- An unfortunate combination of personalities, which prevented team members from finding their preferred team roles, led to unsuccessful teams.
- The most damaging team members were those whose team contribution was seen as a liability rather than an asset, or those who were seen to be deliberate wreckers.
- Team members who were forced into roles which they had neither chosen nor were fitted for became disillusioned, bored, anxious or belligerent.

The experiment revealed that 'winning' teams had a number of qualities:

- The ideal team leader (Chairman) had a strong sense of where he or she was heading, what he or she wanted to achieve, a capacity to welcome **all** contributions from team members without prejudice, and was prepared to accept and take ultimate responsibility. He or she was seen to have slightly above average ability but was not seen as being brilliant.
- There should be one very clever and creative member (Plant). This member was vital to a productive and dynamic team, but it was found to be essential that this member worked with the leader and accepted the leader's ultimate authority.
- Apart from these members there should be a fair spread of mental ability among other members.
- There should be one person with good judgement and discretion, who would be prepared to be pragmatic in giving advice, rather than idealistic or theoretical (Monitor-Evaluator).
- A good spread of team roles should exist, with each member having a useful job and a team role that fitted the member's personality and ability.

Possibly the most important lesson to be learned from this work is that those forced into undertaking tasks or roles for which they are patently unfitted cannot be blamed for failing. The good manager knows the strengths and weaknesses of each team member. All too often the weaknesses are held against a staff member, and are in fact not allowable despite the compensating strengths. As a result, members tend to try to conceal weaknesses and agree to undertake tasks with which they are unfamiliar, have imperfectly learned or are temperamentally unsuited for.

The process of team building involves the delegation of task roles fairly and wisely, and to do this the leader must be aware of the dynamics of the group.

Table 3 Useful people to have in teams

Type	Symbol	Typical features	Positive qualities	Allowable weaknesses
Company Worker	CW	Conservative, dutiful, predictable	Organizing ability, practical, common sense, hard working, self-discipline	Lack of flexibility, unresponsiveness to unproven ideas
Chairman	CH	Calm, self-confident, controlled	A capacity for treating and welcoming all potential contributors on their merits and without prejudice, a strong sense of objectives	No more than ordinary in terms of intellect or creative ability
Shaper	SH	Highly strung, outgoing, dynamic	Drive and a readiness to challenge inertia, ineffectiveness, complacency or self-deception	Proneness to provocation, irritation and impatience
Plant	PL	Individualistic, serious minded, unorthodox	Genius, imagination, intellect, knowledge	Up in the clouds, inclined to disregard practical details or protocol
Resource Investigator	RI	Extroverted, enthusiastic, curious, communicative	A capacity for contacting people and exploring anything new, an ability to respond to challenge	Liable to lose interest once the initial fascination has passed
Monitor-Evaluator	ME	Sober, unemotional, prudent	Judgement, discretion, hard headedness	Lacks inspiration or the ability to motivate others
Team Worker	TW	Socially orientated, rather mild, sensitive	An ability to respond to people and to situations, and to promote team spirit	Indecisiveness at moments of crisis
Completer-Finisher	CF	Painstaking, orderly, conscientious, anxious	A capacity for follow through, perfectionism	A tendency to worry about small things, a reluctance to 'let go'

From: R. Meredith Belbin, *Management Teams: Why They Succeed or Fail* (Heinemann: 1984).

1.1 The effectiveness of groups

Size

Large groups of up to 20 members will obviously provide a greater diversity of skills and knowledge, but the possibility of individual participation is reduced. The **ideal working group** is thought to be between 5 and 8. The **ideal command group** is between 10 and 11.

Composition

Homogeneous groups, of those holding similar attitudes, beliefs and values, will find it easier to arrive at a consensus of opinion. The problem is that decisions suggested may not be challenged because the group is too comfortable and unwilling to disturb the happy atmosphere by raising controversial subjects.

Heterogeneous groups, containing a mix of personalities and opinions, tend to be uncomfortable 'hives' where conflict is common but ideas and alternatives abound. They are generally more productive than homogeneous groups.

Groups containing too many creative and 'difficult' members will produce ideas but rarely arrive at decisions.

Ergonomics

The size of the group chosen to perform the work should never be determined by the size of the room available for meetings! The rule of thumb should be that the room is appropriate to the group, and that the group should be comfortable in it.

Long, rectangular tables and imposing upright chairs are much favoured for hierarchically organised groups such as board meetings. They can also be used to awe and impress those attending meetings, and are sometimes deliberately used with this in mind. Comfortable armchairs, arranged in a circle with a low coffee table bearing refreshments in the middle, may give a friendly appearance, but may not be conducive to positive, dynamic decision making.

Most working groups will prefer to have a table to facilitate writing and to enphasise the need for concentration on the task in hand. A circular table will ensure free exchange of views and is considered to be most suitable for an unstructured group.

1.2 Team development

It has been observed that all groups go through similar processes in their evolution. One model that describes this process suggests that there are four main stages:

Forming

The group come together and seek to get acquainted. This is a time for introductions and for social interactions.

Storming

Having learned the superficial details of their colleagues, members now seek to discover much more about them. Where will support come from? Who is likely to be difficult? What are the hidden agendas? Most important of all, where do **I** fit in? There is a struggle for power within the group, however politely it may be conducted. Members need to know what their roles and tasks will be.

Norming

Once the working relationships are established the atmosphere becomes less tense and issues can be dealt with openly.

Performing

The group begins to do the work for which it was constituted. Few teams progress in an orderly manner through these stages. Commonly, teams return again and again to the early stages, and the coming and going of members breaks up established patterns of behaviour and returns them to 'storming' behaviour.

The loss of a member, or the break up of a team, leads to one further stage in the process – mourning.

1.3 The role of groups

Organisations use groups to distribute, manage and control work. The team tasks demanded by the organisation are:

- problem solving and decision making
- testing organisational decisions
- information processing
- opinion and statistical data collection
- negotiating and resolving conflict.

They also anticipate that team work will increase commitment to the enterprise and will involve everyone in the objectives of the enterprise.

Individuals use groups:

- to achieve personal agendas
- to establish their self concepts
- to satisfy their social needs.

Team leaders use groups:

- to interpret the objectives, decisions and policies of the organisation to team members
- to seek help and support in carrying them out
- to seek help in local decision making and problem solving.

2. Delegating

How often have you heard (or said) 'If you want a thing done properly, do it yourself!' How often have you impatiently pushed a struggling colleague aside saying 'Oh! Come on, let **me** do it or we'll be here all day!' Do you behave like this? If so:

- Have you failed to instruct your subordinate adequately in the job you have asked your subordinate to do? If so, then that person is bound to fail from the outset.
- Are you reluctant to 'let go' of that particular job? Are you, as a result, half-

hoping that your subordinate will fail because it will reinforce your feeling that no one can do it as well as you can?

- Are you afraid to see someone do the job in a new way, or are you perhaps afraid that the new way will prove better?
- Are you afraid that if you delegate, you will no longer be 'on top' of the work?

2.1 Planned delegation

The manager who rushes into a subordinate's office on Friday and says 'You do know I'm away on Monday and you'll be doing my work don't you?' is a menace, and moreover does not do him or herself any favours by such a casual and careless attention to responsibilities. A manager who adds 'Leave all the decisions until I get back, just keep things ticking over' isn't really a manager at all. However, because few of us are prepared to admit that we can't cope for any reason, the response we will usually give is 'Yes, of course Miss Bungler, leave it to me!'

Subordinates should be taught elements of the manager's job from the outset. But **which** elements? To decide this:

- Look at and write down the objectives of your job.
- Keep a record over (say) a month of all the tasks you perform and the number of times (daily or weekly) you perform them.
- Compare objectives and tasks and decide which tasks you could delegate **without** adversely affecting your objectives. There will be some tasks that you cannot delegate:
  - those beyond the ability of the subordinate
  - those of a confidential nature, restricted to your level of management
  - those concerning the discipline of other subordinates
- When you have decided what tasks you may **safely** delegate:
  - instruct the subordinate **carefully** in the task
  - allow the subordinate to carry it out for a short period of time while you are there to offer help if it becomes **absolutely necessary. Do not:**
  - Breathe down your subordinate's neck while the task is being done. Delegation means handing over not only the task but with it the authority to make decisions and to choose options.
  - Suddenly snatch back the task from your surbordinate if you think it is not being done properly. Sit down together and consider the actions and decisions, and help your subordinate see where things are going wrong.

Rules of delegation	(1) Ultimate accountability for all work, including that of subordinates, rests with the manager, so preparation for delegation must be thorough. (2) Delegation helps subordinates learn. It is a part of career development and improves team morale. (3) All delegation involves risk, but the rewards are worth the risks, which are minimised by careful coaching. (4) Despite careful preparation, mistakes will occur, from time to time. Learn from them. **Do not take fright and stop delegating.**

3. Meetings and committees

One result of the changing culture of organisations, from the concept of management by one 'boss' to that of team management, has been the proliferation of meetings, committees or boards, many of which are of doubtful value. Managers in industry are said to spend as much as one-half of their time in meetings, yet many of them appear very cynical of their efficiency. Professor Galbraith, of time and motion fame, said 'Meetings are indispensable when you don't want to do anything!' Sir Bernard Cocks described a committee as 'A cul-de-sac down which ideas are lured and then quietly strangled!' If these two pundits are correct, **why** do managers at every level appear so eager to attend meetings? Perhaps a look at the many functions which committees serve may help answer this question.

3.1 Functions of meetings

- To exchange information and ideas.
- To make group decisions, or to influence decision making elsewhere.
- To make group judgements.
- To solve problems.
- To make recommendations.
- To co-ordinate a number of teams, disciplines or professions and to ensure that they are all involved in the decision-making process.
- To aid in group development and cohesiveness, and to motivate through participation.
- To avoid personal responsibility or decision making and the investment of too much authority in any one person.

Exercise 13

(1) What meetings do you attend? How often do you attend? What are their functions? What do **you** gain from attending?
(2) Why do you attend meetings?
   (a) Because you have been told to do so?
   (b) Because you need to know what other members think or intend to do?
   (c) Because it would lower your status if you were not invited?
   (d) Because you wish to influence management or the organisation?
   (e) Because it gives you an hour or so away from the 'shop floor'?
   (f) For purely social reasons; it's nice to meet your colleagues for a chat.
   (g) For other reasons; think them out for yourself.

Try and define **honestly** to yourself what your motives are. Do not be ashamed of them. They are all legitimate. If you know what they are you will be more effective in your contributions.

3.2 Kinds of meetings

Line or staff committees

'Line' committees are those that make decisions which affect the manager's subordinates. 'Staff' committees are advisory, offering suggestions and/or recommendations to senior management.

Formal/informal meetings and groups

Formal meetings include:

- board meetings
- team officers' meetings (for example, district or possibly unit meetings)
- all committees.

The various types of committees are:

- Executive committees, which are elected at an Annual General Meeting (AGM) and are formed to administer a society or other group of that kind.
- Standing committees, which are appointed by other committees to study and administer different sections of the work on a permanent basis (for example, finance, general purposes, welfare, etc.).
- *Ad hoc* committees or subcommittees, which are set up by executive or standing committees to carry out a specific piece of work. They are small and consist of very specialist members, and they cease to exist when their work is completed.
- Joint committees, which are formed to bring together members from several other committees with similar terms of reference. Their brief is to share information, prevent overlap of work and explore joint working ventures.
- In addition to these committees, which are inter-organisational, there are also national committees.

Informal meetings include:

- many team meetings and some unit meetings
- peer group meetings.

Groups can be:

- therapeutic groups (for example, AA, drug therapy and support groups)

- pressure groups, brought together to achieve a particular objective
- discussion groups (usually social in nature)
- problem-solving groups
- study groups
- T-groups (leaderless groups set up to look at behaviour as it occurs).

Informal meetings may have a leader or be leaderless. If they have a leader, it is the responsibility of the leader to:

- plan the meetings
- know and greet the members
- open and close the meetings
- introduce speakers
- guide any discussion
- plan future work.

3.3 The 'mechanics' of meetings

The agenda

An agenda is a formal list of those matters which are to be discussed at the meeting. It should be sent out at least 10 days before the meeting, so that the attenders will know what is to be discussed and have time to prepare answers which they may be asked to give, and to ensure that they know where the various items may lead.

When you receive the agenda, read it **well in advance** so that you can 'do your homework'. Do not leave it until the evening before, or to read on the train or bus on the way to the meeting. At that point, the notes you want will **not** be where you want them! Nor can you contact other members to find out where your support will be.

The agenda is sent out with:

- minutes of the last meeting (**read carefully**)
- copies of correspondence
- other papers or reports.

It gives the **date, time** and **place** of the meeting (make sure you are going on the right day, at the right time and to the right place!)

Specimen agenda format	(1) Title
	(2) Apologies for absence (**always** let the Secretary know, either by telephone or in writing, if you cannot attend)
	(3) Minutes of the last meeting
	(4) Matters arising
	(5) Correspondence
	(6) To receive reports from
	(7) To consider
	(8) Any other business (try to avoid raising matters under this heading, and beware of others doing so, as it is one way of springing surprises on unprepared members)
	(9) Date, time and venue of next meeting (usually decided with members at the end of the meeting, unless the meeting takes place on a regular, previously decided, time).

Hidden agendas

In addition to the agenda sent out to the committee members, everyone who attends will have their own 'agenda'. While this is quite legitimate, the member may or may not be prepared to reveal what this agenda is.

Some hidden agendas are of an innocent nature – 'I will try to make sure that this meeting does not last too long so that I can get away early.' This may result in the member trying to block discussion. However, some hidden agendas can be destructive and result in the deliberate blocking of decisions so that the member can manipulate others. An able Chairman will recognise and help to reveal the true purpose of the member, perhaps by confrontation and saying something like 'Mrs Brown is there anything which you could tell us to explain your reservations on this matter?' or the Chairman might ask everyone round the table to comment in turn.

Although it is principally the job of the Chairman to deal with hidden agendas, every member of every committee should be aware of their presence and should learn how to work with them. It is rarely helpful to confront someone in an antagonistic manner, although sometimes the half-joking remark 'I think Bill has something in mind he isn't telling us!' may produce some result, even if it is only to show Bill that he has been rumbled!

Agendas for informal groups and meetings

The habit that unfortunately some groups have of arriving in a room at 9 am every Monday morning for a meeting, with no idea of what they will discuss, how long they will be there or who might or might not attend, is to be deplored, and is the hallmark of poor management practices. If such a group has a leader, then it is the responsibility of that leader to circulate a **short** agenda, at least the day before the meeting. This need only be a slip of paper listing the items for discussion.

Items for discussion – **Monday 10 May 10.30 am**	(1) Staffing problems – Mrs Jones (2) Transport difficulties – Mr Higgs (3) Information The meeting will finish promptly at 11.30 am or before.

Another way of collecting items for discussion is to leave a notebook in a central place, so that any interested member can add an item for discussion.

It is important, at the beginning of every meeting, to set a time limit to the meeting. This may be determined by the time of trains, or by the need of member(s) to leave for another meeting or appointment.

Minutes

Minutes are defined as **an accurate and condensed report of what took place at the last meeting.** But beware! They can be so subtly worded as to report what the Chairman or Secretary would **like** to have seen take place! **So read them carefully.** If you subsequently find yourself subscribing to policies you do not agree with and did not support, you have only yourself to blame! This does not mean that you are being asked to subscribe to conspiratorial theories, or being asked to be unduly sceptical as to the motives of all Chairmen. Most of them are honest and meticulous in their reporting. However, meetings are not always as straightforward as they appear, and people can make genuine mistakes. Be prepared to challenge what is written when the item 'matters arising' is announced.

Hints on meetings	(1) Always take very brief notes of what was agreed in a meeting and of who agreed to do it, **especially if you agreed to do something.** Make sure you know precisely what is wanted of you. (2) If you are not clear as to what you are to do, **ask.** (3) Read your minutes **as soon as you get them.** (4) If you think there are errors, **say so.** Remember, once the minutes are accepted, they cannot be changed and are a permanent record. (5) If you cannot attend the meeting to object, write to the Chairman and ask for the issue to be raised.

3.4 The work of the Chairman and Secretary

Skills and qualities of the Chairman

- Must have a calm and friendly personality which will encourage even the most timid member to contribute.

- Must be able to control the other members and have sufficient presence to make this clear to the members.
- Must be able to paraphrase and summarise accurately, picking out, from a plethora of ideas, those suggestions and comments which are of real value and importance.
- Must be in absolute control of him or herself at all times.

The Chairman's role

- Has a sound knowledge of rules on matters of procedure.
- Is responsible for the conduct of the meeting, sets its tone and determines the boundaries of the discussion.
- Ensures that the work of the meeting is carried out, takes precedence over other members and has the casting vote.
- Controls the meeting by ensuring that all comments go 'through the chair' (**all** members address **all** comments to the Chairman and do not argue with each other across the table). The form of address is 'Chairman' or 'Madam Chairman' ('Madam Chair' is sometimes used today) 'I should like to tell Mr Higgs that . . .'
- Works closely with the Secretary and ensures that he or she knows what is agreed and who is to take action.
- Must be impartial. The point at which the Chairman gives the casting vote should be the first time that anyone has any inkling of the Chairman's feelings on any particular subject.
- Is there to control, listen and assist, and **not to dominate.**
- Ensures that meetings begin on time, proceed at a reasonable pace, and end formally and on time.

Skills and qualities of the Secretary

- Should be a good organiser and administrator.
- Should be interested in the process and content of meetings.
- Must be able to keep accurate notes of meetings, by being able to **listen** and to write down words and phrases which will later help to write the minutes, and **must be absolutely sure of what was decided.** If this is not clear, the Secretary should ask the Chairman **at the time,** so that the member concerned can confirm.

The Secretary's role

- Decides whether the meeting is necessary, what its objectives are and who, apart from regular members, should attend.
- Decides who else needs to know, and how much they need to know. Occasionally people who do not attend the meetings receive the minutes and agendas. Only those who have a real need to know should be given this information.
- Prepares the agenda and decides:
  - roughly how long each item will take
  - what outcome is required — a decision or a recommendation
  - what contribution each member is likely to make.
- Briefs the Chairman as to:
  - the objectives of the meeting
  - the objectives of each agenda item, what support there is likely to be and any background information.
- Assembles any necessary papers and sends them out with the agenda with a list of any special people who may be present.
- Makes all 'domestic arrangements'; cloakroom availability, telephones, how messages can be passed to members during the meeting, refreshments, heat, light, arrangement of chairs, any equipment needed (for example, overhead projectors).
- Makes sure that the room is arranged so that everyone can see and be seen.
- Ensures that writing materials are available.
- Prepares papers that are to be tabled.

Tabling	The tabling of papers should be discouraged except in the most exceptional circumstances. Members are at a distinct disadvantage when confronted with tabled papers, as they cannot then read them carefully and prepare a reasoned response. In these circumstances they should ask for decisions to be deferred until a later meeting, or request a period of silence so that the paper can be read.
	Where the author of tabled papers is asked to 'speak to them', it is possibly less dangerous, but members should also view this approach with great caution.

3.5 Members of committees – skills and roles

It is obvious that the Chairman and the Secretary of any committee are very important people, but their work depends on the co-operation and work of the members. Members must be well informed, not only in their own subjects, but also in the work, objectives and constitution of the committee of which they are members. It is essential that agendas are read, preparations for meetings are carefully made, minutes also carefully read, and any action called for by a member conscientiously carried out.

Members must put their points of view **clearly** and **succinctly** and be prepared to listen to the opinions of other members. It has been said that minds are like parachutes, they only function when open! There is little use in attending a meeting if you have already decided that under no circumstances can you be persuaded to change your mind or your opinion. If an argument appears reasonable, and is obviously in the interests of the organisation, it must at least be given consideration.

A good member will be aware of the behaviour of others and what it signifies, and will be experienced enough to look for and recognise hidden agendas in others, and to recognise his or her own!

A word about lobbying – the attempt to influence another or others in the formation of policy. It happens! Do not let it take you by surprise. It is a legitimate activity, and you may wish to further your own objectives by finding out who is likely to support you. There are those who become known for their over vigorous lobbying. These people are often seen as manipulative and devious, so carry on your lobbying discreetly, and only when necessary to achieve the objectives of the organisation.

Roles of meetings	A meeting is a place where:
	• information is exchanged
	• the articulate can impress others by their brilliance!
	• managers make judgements about others, often unfairly
	• the reactions of others to your ideas can be tested out
	• you can support your friends and score off your enemies!
	• managers can be persuaded to do something in public which in private they would resist.

Times to fight

● When the case being made is ethically wrong.
● When the cost (not always in money) will be too great.
● When it is obvious that the proposed action is impossible in the time or manner suggested, or with the available resources.
● When you suspect the integrity of another.
● When you do not feel that the case has been made, or is based on inaccuracies.

Times for flight

● When the point is insignificant and you can gain a more important point later.
● When it is obvious that no one else will support you.
● When you are proved to be wrong.

3.6 Blocking communications in and between groups

Most of these are defence mechanisms and can be distracting and destructive.

Pairing and colluding

Two members of the group carrying on a conversation during a meeting or, worse, passing notes, can be very disruptive. It is immature behaviour and usually indicates an attempt to opt out of the meeting. Occasionally members of a group conspire to share jokes, looks or references obscure to other members of the group. This can also be very disruptive.

Jargon

This is acceptable only if it is understood by all members.

Distracting and irrelevancy

This is accomplished by casting 'red herrings' into the discussion or by going off at a tangent on another subject, by changing the subject or by ignoring what has just been said.

Opting out

Nothing is more irritating than a person who leans back with arms folded looking out of the window or at the ceiling. Other members are made to feel that what they are contributing is of little value. Another way of opting out is to draw elaborated doodles.

Intellectualising

This is a common ploy of the 'expert' who chooses to dazzle the audience or to demonstrate brilliance. It is also used to prevent exploration of feelings which may be painful. The opposite of this is to speak **only** of feelings and emotions, and to ignore pragmatic issues. Both can be a form of flight from the work which has to be done.

Rescuing

Replying for others, explaining their statements, justifying their responses or analysing their motives is rationalised by claiming that they need help. However, what it accomplishes is probably counterproductive, as it prevents that person from understanding his or her own hidden agenda, and thus learning about him or herself. It tends to block more than a superficial level of work. It is sometimes an indication of a member trying to take over the leadership by keeping all communication centred on him or herself rather than going through the Chair.

Divide and rule

This is the sharing of different confidences with individuals in the group and indicating that you are telling them something which you are not willing to share with anyone else. This encourages them to trust you and you only. Thus cabals are formed within the group, which can ultimately divide or even destroy the group.

Questioning

Repeated questions to one person directs attention away from the work and prevents the person being questioned from examining his or her own agenda.

Scapegoating

This can be the subtle placing of blame for actions that have misfired on to one person in the group, or it can be the whole group colluding to blame the policies of another group for things that go wrong. When a member of the profession that is being blamed in this way is present, that member will feel bound to come to the defence of his or her professional group.

The 'put down'

This is quite destructive and is done to make the doer appear in a more favourable light. It is sometimes used by a person against him or herself, when he or she looks helpless or stupid. It can be used deliberately in this way to indicate that other members are only strong or able when dealing with someone weak or stupid.

Withholding information

This is the refusal to divulge what you know, or implying that you know something others do not. A great personal status builder.

Stereotyping

This involves members conniving to complain about groups whose culture or ways are different.

4. Behaviour in groups

Psychologists have long taken a great interest in the way in which people behave in groups, how this behaviour affects others and how to categorise behaviours. Two psychologists who have made a special study of behaviour and how it may be categorised are Rackham and Morgan[3] who, after much testing and refining, identified 13 categories of behaviour exhibited by those working in groups. These categories fall into four main groups:

(1) **Initiating behaviours** – proposing, building.
(2) **Reacting behaviours** – supporting, disagreeing, defending/attacking, blocking/difficulty stating, open behaviour.
(3) **Clarifying behaviours** – testing understanding, summarising, seeking information, giving information.
(4) **Others** – bringing in, shutting out.

4.1 How the identification of behaviour categories can help

It has already been shown that the practice of attending meetings is a skill and that there are many pitfalls for the unwary. As a corollary of this, it was proposed that those participating in this art form should be as aware as possible of how others are likely to behave, and how such behaviour might affect the ability of the organisation, the group and the member to achieve his or her objectives.

The 13 behaviour categories would undoubtedly heighten awareness in this area, but it is not easy to arrive at a simple analysis of what is going on in a series of meetings. Rackham and Morgan suggest that observations should be made over a number of meetings for such an analysis and Figure 9 demonstrates how the behaviours exhibited could be recorded. It may not be possible, for a number of reasons, to carry out such a systematic evaluation. However, it **should** be possible to view the proceedings of meetings with a heightened awareness and to get some feel for the behavioural patterns of members.

4.2 Using the Rackham and Morgan categories

Initiating behaviours

Proposing is the putting forward of new suggestions or a new course of action. For example, 'Let's transfer Miss Smith's work to Miss Brown' or 'How would it be if we cut out the weekly meeting?' Looking back at the personalities the Henley–Cambridge work suggested as useful team members, it can be seen that the most likely people to make proposals are the **Plant** and the **Resource Investigator.** Many 'proposers' tend to be enthusiasts, eager to offer new ideas, but once they have made the proposal their minds are off chasing new ideas, leaving someone else to follow up the work. Do not condemn them for this facility. They are sometimes rather contemptuously referred to as 'butterflies', but they are vital to an energetic and productive team. Don't be too hard on the apparently 'way out' suggestions either. They can at times be more

Date _____ Observer **N.R.** Group **Policy Committee**

Task **Meeting 3** Observation time Start 0900 / Finish 1200 Total (mins) 180

Name (Note Chairman)	Bill	John	Den	Dick	Chas	Total
Proposing	HHt HHt / HHt HHt / HHt HHt	HHt HHt / II	HHt HHt / HHt II		II	59
Building		HHt II	IIII			11
Supporting	HHt HHt HHt / HHt HHt / HHt IIII	HHt HHt / HHt III	III	III	IIII	62
Disagreeing	HHt HHt / HHt HHt / HHt I	III		I	HHt HHt / HHt III	48
Defending/attacking	HHt HHt / HHt III				HHt HHt / IIII	32
Blocking/difficulty stating	III	I	III	I	HHt HHt / HHt II	25
Open		II	I	III		6

Name (Note Chairman)	Bill	John	Den	Dick	Chas	Total
Testing understanding	I	HHt HHt / IIII	HHt HHt / II	II		29
Summarising	I	HHt IIII	HHt HHt / IIII		I	25
Seeking information	HHt II	HHt HHt / HHt HHt / III	HHt HHt / HHt IIII	III	III	55
Giving information	HHt HHt HHt / HHt HHt HHt / HHt HHt HHt / III	HHt HHt IIII	HHt II	HHt HHt II	HHt HHt HHt / HHt HHt HHt / IIII	115
Shutting out	HHt HHt HHt / HHt HHt HHt / HHt HHt HHt / HHt HHt HHt / III	HHt II	HHt HHt HHt / HHt I		HHt HHt HHt / HHt HHt	116
Bringing in	II	HHt HHt / I	HHt HHt / III		I	27
Total	231	121	114	25	119	610

Figure 9 Behavioural analysis of a group at work
From: N. Rackham and T. Morgan, *Behaviour Analysis in Training*, page 150, 1977.

sensible than they at first appear. There is always the **Completer-Finisher** to follow up!

Building is usually a behaviour that extends or develops a proposal made by another. The **Team Worker** and the **Shaper** seem to fit into this category. For example, 'And your idea would be even better if we tried it out with Dr Jones first!' or 'You have suggested that we close the annex. I've got some ideas as to how we might do this.'

Reacting behaviours

In **supporting,** one member makes a conscious and direct declaration of support for another person and his or her concepts. For example, 'I'd go along with that' or 'That seems to make sense.' This is probably the **Company Worker** – if he or she is sure that the idea or the person needs to be supported. Both builders and supporters are useful people to have in your corner, and are essential in making the committee or meeting a dynamic entity.

In **disagreeing,** a member makes a conscious and direct declaration of disagreement. For example, 'I don't agree with that idea. It's not something we could do here very easily.' This is the **Company Worker** who has just been offered a new and unproven idea and thinks it is a bit rocky! Listen to this member, who knows the field, but don't let him or her interfere with really tenable ideas just because he or she is afraid to try them out. Remember, change for its own sake may not be good.

In contrast to the member who disagrees about **issues,** the **defender/attacker** is much more personal. The behaviour of such a person usually involves making value judgements and tends towards the emotional. This type of person is defensive and attacks **people** rather than issues. For example, 'Don't blame me. It wasn't **my** idea!' or 'That's rubbish!'

Blocking/difficulty stating consists of putting objections in the way of progress without offering either any **reasoned** statement to support the objection or an alternative. For example, 'It won't work!' or 'I couldn't possibly accept that.'

The person who demonstrates **open behaviour** exposes him or herself to ridicule or loss of status. It is the opposite of defending/attacking and may include admissions of mistakes made or of inadequacies. It is wise to restrict this form of behaviour to a group where the other members are supportive and not likely to make personal judgements. It is valuable if it can be done in such an atmosphere, as it offers others the opportunity to discuss their own difficulties and, by open discussion, allows for mistakes to be accepted and worked through. It can sometimes be done in a committee meeting in such a way as to elicit sympathy. For example, 'Mea culpa! I've been so frantic lately that it simply slipped my mind, you know how it is?' This acknowledges the shortcoming, but excuses it on the grounds of overwork and suggests that other members might have done just the same!

Clarifying

Testing understanding seeks to establish whether an earlier contribution has been properly understood. For example, 'Can I just check that we are both referring to the same thing here?' The Chairman and the Secretary will both use this kind of behaviour, but it must be stressed again that **any** member should test his or her understanding of what is happening if there is any doubt. Used too often by one member, such behaviour might make others wonder if that person was really listening! The **Completer-Finisher** with his or her painstaking conscientious and anxious personality might do rather more testing than others.

Summarising is mainly a Chairman's behaviour, and duty. For example, 'Members, we have agreed to take immediate action, to ask Mr Brown to co-ordinate the action and to inform every department before any action is begun.'

Seeking information is not quite the same as **testing information,** which asks 'Have I got it right?'. Seeking information asks for facts and opinions or a clarification of them from another. For example, 'Which item of the agenda are we on?' or 'Has that been carefully checked?'

Giving information offers facts and opinions or a clarification of them to others. For example, 'We did much the same thing last year and the results are in the document at page 8' or 'When I said I wasn't concerned, it was because I knew that Miss James's research has proved this action is not damaging.'

Others

Bringing in attempts to involve another person in the discussion or offers that person the opportunity to contribute. For example, 'Mary, you have been very patient while we have all had our say. I wonder whether there is anything you would like to add?' This kind of intervention, usually made by the Chairman, is often necessary to involve someone who is rather diffident about stating feelings or ideas, or has a quiet voice and has been shouted down by others!

Shutting out excludes or reduces another person's contributions. This is sometimes necessary to 'muzzle' the over talkative member, and is usually done by the Chairman. For example, 'Thank you for your very helpful contribution John. Shall we now hear what the other members have to say?' Shutting out by other members is usually done by interrupting. For example, in response to the Chairman's question 'Mary, what do you feel?' Joan says 'What I feel is . . .' Mary is prevented from answering.

Exercise 14

Next time you attend a meeting take some time to observe the behaviour of the other members.

(1) What kind of behaviour can you identify?
(2) What does it tell you about the person concerned?
(3) Watch to see how often that behaviour is repeated by that person.
(4) What kind of behaviour do you think **you** usually demonstrate?

4.3 Analysing interactions

Another desirable piece of information about what happens in committees and meetings is to do with the pattern of exchanges that take place between members:

- Who talks to who?
- How often do they talk to each other?
- Who is the titular leader?
- Is that person the real leader?
- Is there more than one leader?
- Who supports who?
- Who supports **you**?

One way of finding out some of the answers to these questions is to draw a sociogram which describes each interaction (see Figure 10).

It is the wise man who knows that meetings may be very much more than simple social occasions. If you want to be effective in them, become aware of what is going on under your nose!

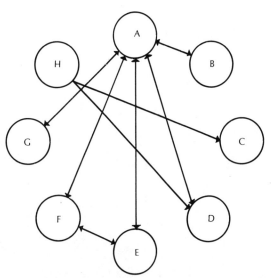

Figure 10 What does this diagram tell you about interactions in this group?

References

1. Peter Drucker, *The Practise of Management*, Pan Management Series (Pan, 1981).
2. R. Meredith Belbin, *Management Teams: Why They Succeed or Fail* (Heinemann, 1984).
3. Neil Rackham and Terry Morgan, *Behaviour Analysis in Training* (McGraw-Hill, 1977).

Suggested further reading

Leland P. Bradford (ed.), *Group Development* (University Associates Inc., 1978).

Annabel Broome, *Managing Change* (Macmillan Education, 1990).

R. Cattell, *Personality and Motivation, Structure and Movement* (Hanah, 1957).

Winston Fletcher, *Meetings, Meetings, How to Manipulate Them and Make Them More Fun* (Michael Joseph, 1983).

Greville Janner, *Janner on Meetings* (Gower, 1986).

Sheila Marson, ed., *Managing Others* (Macmillan Education, 1990).

Neil Rackham, Peter Honey and Michael Colbert, *Developing Interactive Skills* (Wellens Publishing, 1971).

Victor Serebriakoff, *A Guide to Intelligence and Personality Testing* (Parthenon Publishing Group, 1988).

Chapter 5   Staffing

Introduction

This chapter deals with the skills managers employ in dealing with staff in the specific areas of interviewing, assessment and appraisal, and selection and appointment.

The command 'My office, **now!**' is enough to set the heart lurching, the stomach churning and the soul desperately searching for the latest misdemeanour? Certainly it will not be the prelude to a calm, helpful and creative discussion, even in the most innocent or self-confident of people.

Interviewing

Before engaging in any interview, the interviewer needs to ask certain questions.

1. Who do I want to see?

It is surprising how often the wrong person in the organisation is asked for information. Does it **really** make sense to ask the next in line, simply because that person **is** the next in line? In fact, it is probably the 'coal face' worker (CFW) who has the answers. Yet going through the chain of command is common practice in some organisations and works like this:

- Manager A . . . speaks to Manager B
- Manager B . . . speaks to Manager C
- Manager C . . . is briefed by the CFW who relays the answer to B who takes it to A!

What effect does this have?

- The CFW feels undervalued. The CFW knows not only the answer to the question, but also, and probably more importantly, the subtleties and nuances of the situation. The CFW could give valuable information.
- Because the answer has to go through two people before it reaches Manager A, it may well have changed to a lesser or greater degree by the time A gets it.
- Senior management becomes remote and loses touch with the workforce – the 'coal face'.

While it is sometimes necessary to work through the chain of command, such a procedure should always be examined to ensure that it is the most effective way of working.

2. Why do I want to see this person?

Careful preparation **must** be made for **all** interviews. It is helpful to note:

- the objective of the interview
- the point(s) you want to make
- the information you want to elicit.

The **nature** of the interview is also important. It may be:

- investigatory – for example, what is going on in the interviewee's life or work
- information seeking, about work or progress
- disciplinary
- educational and/or developmental
- assessment or appraisal.

And it will determine such matters as:

- where you will hold the interview
- if it is to be a formal or an informal interview
- how long it will take
- if anyone else should be present.

3. How will I conduct the interview?

This will, of course, depend on the kind of interview to be conducted, but there are certain interviewing skills and rules which are common to all interviews:

- Regardless of the nature of the interview, the interviewer will be intent on achieving the set objectives.
- This is best achieved by ensuring that the interview is conducted in an atmosphere free from stress, so that those present can have a constructive and honest exchange of views.
- It is essential that, before engaging in the interview, thought is given to its ambiance and its structure.

3.1 The room layout

Most interviews are conducted in the interviewer's office. This will probably contain a desk, several chairs and possibly a table. It is also likely to contain a mass of papers on desks, chairs and anywhere else there is a space! Clear them away before you begin.

Sitting behind a desk may feel 'safe' and, in certain circumstances – for example, when you wish to emphasise your position as boss – it may be the preferred option. However, it will always inhibit a free exchange to some extent, so some thought should be given to whether it is really necessary.

A table is most useful for working meetings where books and papers need to be spread out. There is nothing worse than having to juggle with pieces of paper that slip to the floor! The same goes for coffee and tea cups. Apart from the danger of spilling coffee over everything, it is very irritating and distracting to balance a cup in one hand while balancing papers on the knees.

Try not to put the interviewee in a chair lower than your own, or facing a sunlit window so that the interviewee has to squint.

Try also to keep a reasonable distance between you and the interviewee so that you are not eyeball to eyeball and bumping knees. Ask the interviewee to choose what chair to sit in. Low, padded, comfortable chairs, found in many offices, are suitable for conversational meetings, where ideas are being exchanged or problems discussed. They are not suitable for working meetings where notes are taken, papers are exchanged or reference must be made to a number of documents. It is wise to consider these points before the interview begins and, if necessary, to book a larger or more suitable room to work in.

3.2 The greeting

One would normally rise to greet anyone coming into a room, for whatever reason, and a handshake signals a warm and friendly atmosphere. No matter how inferior in rank or status the interviewee may be, these common courtesies will put the interviewee at ease and thus enable whatever will transpire to be more comfortably conducted and more productive. Little is ever gained by an irritable or belligerent exchange, and, even if the purpose of the interview is to discipline a subordinate, that person should be given the opportunity to put his or her point of view and explanation.

The offer of refreshments in any interview will help to relieve tension and give the interviewee a feeling that, no matter the reason for the interview, he or she has time to make his or her feelings known, and will at least be listened to courteously and fully.

3.3 Sympathy, empathy and listening

These skills have been discussed in an earlier chapter. It is essential, however, to emphasise that listening, in particular, is most important. Any interview will stretch the listening abilities of the interviewer to the limits, and any interview that has been carried out in a satisfactory manner will leave the interviewer tired and needing a few moments to collect his or her thoughts before returning to other duties.

If the interviewer cannot empathise with the interviewee, it is possible that the interviewer may fail to understand some of the interviewee's more subtle messages.

Sympathy, a very different emotion, is also necessary when there is sadness or anxiety in the life of the interviewee.

All these skills are used to say 'I am with you, I am concerned for you, I care what happens to you.' Their expression **must** be sincere. Insincerity is quickly recognised.

3.4 Non-verbal signals

It is by non-verbal communication that attitudes are so frequently expressed. A grimace quickly suppressed, or an intake of breath at the revelation of something that takes the interviewer by surprise or shocks in some way, is rarely missed. Human beings are amazingly adept at picking up such signals. As it is difficult **not** to react to something that surprises, annoys or offends you, it is probably more useful, and certainly more honest, to acknowledge that, while you do not subscribe to what has been expressed, you nevertheless accept that for the interviewee it **is** acceptable.

Hints on non-verbal signals	Note: ● eye contact ● facial expression ● hand movements ● glances at watch or clock. Avoid: ● glances at watch or clock – however busy you may be ● irritating habits – pen clicking, tapping with the fingers and so on.

3.5 Starting the interview

Following the preliminaries of 'greeting, seating and eating', make sure that the interviewee is comfortable and settled. It may be time consuming to discuss irrelevant matters at the outset, but it is important to ensure that the interview gets off to a good start.

Once the interviewee is at ease, and before the interview begins, it is important to consider its structure together:

● Its purpose and subject matter should be made clear.
● The length of time it will take should be discussed, with reference to any following appointments that either person has, or to other existing time constraints.
● It should be made clear whether a record of the conversation is to be kept, or whether it will be a free discussion in which confidence is respected.

3.6 During the interview

Note taking

It is usually better **not** to take notes in a free-ranging discussion. If notes **are** to be taken, it is important that they are written up later and a copy sent to the interviewee. If notes are **not** taken, but it is important to record the substance of the meeting, notes should be written up as soon as possible following the end of the interview.

Interruptions

Interruptions from outside should **not** occur. Telephone calls should be held during interviews and an engaged sign put on the door to discourage people from entering.

It is also important for the interviewer not to interrupt the interviewee, except in the following circumstances:

- to summarise what has been said in the interests of accuracy
- to bring the interviewee back to the point.

3.7 Ending the interview

It is most productive if an interview ends on a positive and happy note, but unfortunately this is not always possible. If tempers have become strained, it is always better to say something like 'We do not seem to be getting anywhere at the moment. I think it would be helpful if we stopped and got together in a day or so when we have both had time to think over what has been said so far.' If you have said this, however, do not later be drawn back into continuing the argument, but insist that this is what you wish to do, and stick to it.

In all other interviews **summarise** what has been said, checking to ensure that you both agree the main points.

Finally, end, as you began, on a cordial note, possibly shaking hands and thanking the interviewee for coming to see you.

3.8 Following the interview

Make any necessary notes and send a **short** note of the interview to the interviewee, inviting the person to let you know if there are any corrections he or she wishes to make. These notes should contain:

- what was said
- what action was agreed and by whom
- any other details of importance
- any further meeting which was agreed.

If corrections are sent to you, read them carefully to see if you agree, and ensure that they are not so sweeping as to alter the whole thrust of the interview.

4. Points to watch at all interviews

(1) Use of skills:
- listening
- reflecting
- clarifying
- paraphrasing
- summarising
- educating
- problem solving
- making a contract
- terminating.

(2) Use of attributes:
- warmth
- empathy
- genuineness
- non-judgemental attitude
- understanding
- helpfulness.

(3) Was the approach:
- empathic?
- indicative of caring on the part of the interviewer?

(4) Was the interviewer someone who would inspire:
- confidence?
- trust?

(5) How were the verbal and non-verbal skills used?

(6) Did the interviewer get the most possible from the interview? If not, how could the interview have been improved?

(7) What were the **good** points of the interview? The **bad** points?

(8) What was missed?
- cues? Words or phrases used by the interviewee which, regardless of the total message, may have offered some idea of what was in the other person's mind, but were left unsaid.

- use of emotive words? Words such as 'loved' or 'hated' used with great emphasis or used out of context.
- non-verbal signals? Particularly such things as nervousness, attempts at levity not in keeping with the tone of the interview, attempts to cut the interview short and get out.

(9) What kind of voice does the interviewer have? Was it:
- high or squeaky?
- toneless?
- cold or brusque?

(Borrow a tape recorder and listen to yourself. How do you sound to others?)

Exercise 15	(1) If you can do so, practise role playing in interviews using a video record, and then watch the film critically noting the above points.
	(2) Try this exercise for different kinds of interview – assessment, disciplinary, developmental and so on.
	(3) If you do not have access to video equipment, this exercise can be done with an observer who feeds back your weak points honestly and sensitively.
	(4) If your voice appears to you to be rather toneless, or you have irritating verbal habits, consider taking speech training lessons. As a communicator, you may need to ensure that people will not be distracted from **what** you are saying by the **way** you are saying it.

Assessment and appraisal

The term 'appraisal' is used here, although 'staff development and performance review (SD&PR)' is the term currently in use, indicating, as it does, the nature of appraisal as a **positive, developmental** and **non-judgemental** activity. It is, however, pointless changing the **name** of an activity if **attitudes** to it remain unchanged, and no matter how we seek to do this it would be naïve to think that the term 'appraisal' will no longer be used.

This section aims to ensure that nurse managers are reminded of the true nature of SD&PR, and, while the use of the correct term should reinforce the positive aspects of the activity, it is hoped that a revision of the principles of SD&PR will help to correct misconceptions which may exist as to its true purpose.

Both assessment and SD&PR show the developmental aspects of their characters in their objectives which are:

- To identify the strengths and weaknesses of the appraisee by an examination of the appraisee's work since the last SD&PR or assessment.
- To correct the identified weaknesses by offering further training or coaching.
- To ensure that the employee is functioning as effectively and efficiently as possible, and to assist the employee in improving performance, where this is found to be necessary.
- To identify strengths, abilities and potential which could be developed for the benefit of the service.
- To act as an indicator of possible future career moves and paths, by a consideration of the pattern of strengths and weaknesses and how they are developed or dealt with.
- To clarify the expectations of the employer and the employee, to set objectives for future work together and to identify, at the interview, measures by which they can be achieved.

If these are the objectives that appraisers truly employ, it follows that the nature of the activity cannot be punitive or disciplinary in nature, but will be a joint exercise between the appraiser and the appraisee which aims at a positive and rewarding outcome.

1. What SD&PR should do

Nurses are, generally speaking, familiar with SD&PR. They have, through their years as students, had regular and periodic assessments, and the successful attainment of satisfactory assessments may be necessary for the ultimate and successful completion of the nursing qualification. SD&PR **benefits** from this familiarity in that the technique is familiar. It **suffers** from it because the appraisee may tend to see it as a form of examination to be passed. And, as has been seen, SD&PR is in fact something rather different.

Successful SD&PR is the discussion, on a regular basis, of:

- The work of the appraisee since the last appraisal interview.
- The way in which the appraiser and the appraisee work together.
- The problems that the appraisee encounters during work — these may be personal problems or problems with management, colleagues or the organisation itself. Any of these could cause his or her work to suffer.
- How the problems can be solved.
- The good work the appraisee has done, which is now recognised.
- A discussion of the future career of the appraisee.

This forms an agenda for the SD&PR interview, ensuring that the interview is carried out systematically.

2. Preliminaries to the SD&PR interview

- The appraiser should be reminded well in advance that the yearly SD&PR interviews are due. Depending on the number of appraisals to be done, the appraiser should then decide on the number to be undertaken in any one week and the amount of time to be devoted to each interview. It is suggested that three month's notice should be given to the appraiser and that **at least** two hours should be allowed for each SD&PR interview.
- The appraiser should remind the appraisees well in advance that their appraisal will take place on a certain day, time and place. It is suggested that they should be given one month's notice of the interview.
- Appraisees should be asked to do the following:
  - Look out the copy of their last appraisal and decide whether or not the actions agreed have been carried out.
  - Look at their job descriptions and decide whether they have changed or remained static since the last SD&PR review. This is of special importance in view of clinical grading.
  - Prepare for the interview by filling out a specimen SD&PR review form, which they should receive from the appraiser, and which will show how each appraisee sees his or her own work and development.
  - Make a note of any special matters they wish to discuss.

3. The SD&PR interview

The notes on good practice in interviews will, of course, apply but there are some other points to look out for in this very special kind of interview:

- It is essential that the appraiser makes it quite clear at the outset that this is a co-operative discussion. The manager who is best at SD&PR interviewing will recognise that the appraisee may wish to say 'But it is **your** fault that I couldn't do that' and will allow this without feeling threatened or the need to make excuses for what may be his or her shortcomings. To be able to accept that we can all fail at some things and in some ways is a strength, **not** a weakness. It is valuable to the manager to have such feedback, but it cannot be of value if it is not accepted.
- It is essential that the interview is not **interrupted.**
- The interview must not be seen as an opportunity to list all the things the subordinate has been doing wrong for the past year. In fact, nothing that is said about the appraisee's performance should come as a surprise. A subordinate should be told of his or her progress regularly throughout the year. The SD&PR interview is merely a time when appraiser and appraisee can look at their work together in depth and see how it can be improved.
- At the end of the exercise **both** parties should feel good and know that what they have discussed has been constructive and helpful to both of them.
- The SD&PR interview is a test of the trust and regard the appraisee has in his or her boss. The appraiser is also being appraised and so has a unique opportunity to judge from the reactions of the appraisee how his or her work is regarded by subordinates.

SD&PR interview checklist	<ul><li>Have the forms and instructions gone out well in advance?</li><li>Have you given sufficient time to complete the exercise comfortably and without appearing rushed?</li><li>Have you ensured that you will not be interrupted?</li><li>Check on 'points to watch at all interviews' (page 58).</li><li>Has the appraisee been trained in SD&PR techniques? This must be done **before** the first interview.</li><li>Make sure that the appraisee has brought: – a job description – a copy of the last appraisal.</li><li>Go over the job description checking whether any of the tasks have changed or no longer apply.</li><li>Look at the tasks which, at the last interview, it was agreed the appraisee would try to achieve.</li><li>If they have not been achieved, why not? It could be: – the appraisee's fault – is extra training needed? – your fault – invite the appraisee to tell you if this is so. You may have a very good reason for your failure, but try not to make excuses. – the fault of the organisation – lack of money or of interest. If so, say why.</li><li>Ask the appraisee about any weaknesses and what you can do to help – extra training, acting up, visiting another unit.</li><li>Ask the appraisee about strengths and discuss how these could be best used.</li><li>Tell the appraisee what **you** see as strengths and weaknesses, inviting comment. **Listen** to what the appraisee has to say and do not be too quick to brush off these comments as mere excuses for poor work. Your function is to help, not to condemn.</li><li>Agree the special tasks (3 to 4 at most) which you both feel would be achievable and desirable for the next year. These should be written down on the special form provided and a copy kept by both appraiser and appraisee.</li><li>Discuss future career plans and offer any help which can be reasonably given. This may consist of referring the appraisee to a place where further information can be obtained, or it can entail a careful examination of the reasons why the appraisee wishes to make that choice and whether the appraisee's particular strengths would be suitable in that area. **Try not to advise.** Rather, **seek to help the appraisee look realistically at the options so that an informed choice can be made** by the **appraisee.**</li><li>End the interview on a positive and encouraging note.</li></ul>

4. Following the interview

SD&PR does not end with the interview. Following it, a number of actions are necessary:

- A note of the interview must be sent **in confidence** to the appraisee.
- This should include a special note of what was agreed should be done by appraiser and appraisee.
- A copy of the final form should be sent to the appraisee. (In some cases the copy is not sent, but is shown to the appraisee at the end of the interview. The important thing is that what you have said about the appraisee has been seen and agreed, or if it has not been agreed, a note to that effect should be appended at the bottom of the form.)
- Any extra training agreed as being desirable should now be arranged with the Personnel Department, and other forms of development arranged.
- If the job has changed, a new job description should be sent to the appraisee for agreement.

Exercise 16	You have in your team a young man who is destined for a senior management post, if you can persuade him that he must look more clearly at his personal relationships. He tends to be somewhat abrasive with subordinates and cannot make easy relationships. You are about to have your yearly SD&PR interview with him. (1) What preparations would you make prior to the interview? (2) Role play in groups of threes: A, B and C.<ul><li>A acts the part of the appraiser</li><li>B acts the part of the interviewee</li><li>C acts the part of the observer.</li></ul>

C should look out for the manner of the interview, its success or failure, and how much the young man would have been helped by it. During the role play C should not speak. This role play would be most profitably done if video equipment is used.

(3) What kind of help do you think could usefully be offered to someone with personality problems of the kind described?

5. Confidentiality and custody of forms

What occurs during SD&PR interviews is, of course, confidential between the appraiser and the appraisee. This raises questions of where the forms should be kept and what they should be used for in the future.

5.1 Storage and use of forms

It is usually the custom for the part of the completed SD&PR form dealing with training needs to be retained by the Personnel Department. Occasionally all of the form is retained by the Personnel Department, or the Senior Nurse Manager may keep custody. The appraisee should have a **complete** copy of the form.

It is also the custom for the nurse manager to use such forms as a guide when a summary of a nurse's career is needed, on leaving that employing authority.

It is usually agreed that the forms should never be used directly for references.

It is important that these forms should be used in a **positive** manner to give guidance on the training required, not only for individuals, but also to provide an overview of the kind of training that nurses of similar grades would find most useful.

The forms themselves will vary from district to district – but the National Staff Committee for Nurses and Midwives in May 1977 developed a system and forms carefully researched by Deborah Jones and Anne Rogers of the Polytechnic of Central London, and that scheme, updated, widened in scope and adapted to local needs, is still in use in many places today.

It is useful to review SD&PR schemes from time to time and to think carefully about their relevance, the appropriateness of the questions they ask and what their objectives are.

6. Clinical grading

SD&PR will be especially important in view of this relatively new development in nursing.

Appraisers must be aware of their responsibilities and of the skills which must be considered at interview with staff when grades are awarded.

Selection and appointment of staff

Unless a team is carefully chosen and balanced, it will not function adequately. It seems strange, therefore, that all too often those who have to work together are chosen and come together in a working situation without having met before. Thus a Ward Sister who is allocated a Staff Nurse or Junior Sister that he or she has never met may take an instant dislike to that person. If such unfortunate appointments are to be avoided, it would seem rational to ensure that nurse managers take part in making appointments. At the very least they should be given the opportunity to meet with and give opinions on new appointees with whom they must work. For this reason, it is necessary that every member of the team is aware of the principles of selection and appointment, and how **good** appointments are made.

Most nurse managers will, at some time, wish to apply for other posts, and for this reason this section describes interviewing techniques from the point of view of the appointing committee, as well as from the point of view of the applicant.

1. Making appointments

1.1 Preliminaries to appointments

Unless the post is a new one, you should always determine whether the post is still needed. It can happen that, as the organisation changes, the need for certain posts ceases.

The next step is to see if the post needs to be re-assessed. When we looked at appraisal, we saw that an individual often tailors a post to suit his or her own personality and abilities. Such changes may subtly alter the original intentions of the post. Thus, when the post becomes vacant, this is the time to re-assess how it should be carried out in the interests of the organisation.

Having drawn up the intentions of the post, the next step is to outline the profile of the person to occupy the post. What kind of person is wanted? What **must** this person have to fit into the team? (Remember the theory of the Henley–Cambridge teams who looked at allowable weaknesses and the need to fit the team together so that everyone worked to their best potential.)

It may well be that the ideal candidate is already in the organisation, willing and able to fill the post. There are positive and negative points for such a decision:

- Why go to the cost of looking 'outside' if it is not really necessary?
- It may be good practise for candidates to attend interviews, but are we in the business of providing such a costly exercise?
- There might be an even better candidate outside the organisation, but if someone is functioning well, knows the other people concerned and is doing a good job, why 'rock the boat'?
- Fresh blood may provide a challenge to the organisation and improve it.

All these points must be considered before a decision to advertise widely is made.

Having decided what the post is and what kind of person is wanted to fill that post, advertisements are placed in papers and/or journals which are most likely to attract the kind of person you are looking for. These advertisements should describe the post (give the role specification), the kind of person being sought and such details as salary, opportunities available for career enhancement and training, and any other matters that will help applicants decide whether they fit the profile of the possible candidate. The advertisement should also give the final date for acceptance of applications.

When applications are received they should be acknowledged at once. Nothing is more disturbing for applicants than to send off an application which vanishes without trace into some secret administrative conclave. Applicants cannot decide whether it will appear 'pushy' to ring up and ask if it has been received or whether, if they don't, it will look as though they don't really care!

Between the placing of the advertisement and the shortlisting, assessors are sought. It is important that the assessors are well briefed as to what kind of applicant is being sought, the kind of post that is being filled and the ethos of the particular area in which the post exists. Assessors are non-voting members, present at the interview to ensure 'fair play'. Assessors have one further duty, that of helping the candidates.

On reception of all applications, shortlisting takes place. It is desirable for assessors to be involved in this process. Candidates on the short list are then informed and are given details of:

- when the interview, if there is to be one, will be held
- the time of the interview
- roughly how long it will take
- how to get to the place concerned, with maps if possible
- details of trains, buses and car parking.

Applicants should be offered the opportunity to look at the place where they might be working, and perhaps invited to an informal meeting with their future colleagues. This will give both applicants and future colleagues the opportunity to decide whether it would be desirable to continue with the interview.

Those applicants who are not shortlisted should be written to with an explanation of why their application has not been successful. Such refusals can be very discouraging, and may leave applicants unsure of themselves and feeling that they should not apply for further posts. It is worth giving some thought to the letter to be written to applicants. It should re-assure them that their having been refused is **not** due to their unsuitability for posts in general, but simply that, in the view of the advertisers, they do not fit the specific profile of the candidate being sought **for that particular post.**

Following shortlisting the references of the applicants to be interviewed are sent for, and the interview arranged.

1.2 The appointment interview

The main point to remember when carrying out appointment interviews is that their purpose is to appoint the best candidate. That is, the person who fits most aptly into the team, fits the profile of the appointee sought and is best able to carry out the tasks of the post.

It follows, therefore, that the appointing committee will wish to conduct the interview in an atmosphere that enables the candidates to demonstrate their abilities most effectively, and does not cause undue stress. There is a school of thought that tends to the idea that, as the appointee will often be in stressful situations during the normal course of work, it would be helpful to see how the individual copes with stress at interview. While this may be an understandable point of view, it is flawed in that the two kinds of stress are rarely synonymous. While one candidate can cope with interview stress, but may fold under long, drawn out occupational stress, another may find the notion of interviews and/ or examinations very difficult to come to terms with.

All the rules previously discussed for carrying out interviews apply here, but there are some additional ones that should be noted:

- Rather than having **all** the candidates waiting in one room, ready to be called one at a time, it is better to apportion a definite time for each interview.
- The appointing committee should not be too large. Nothing is more daunting than to be ushered through a door to find a huge table behind which there seem to be dozens of people watching you.
- This journey from door to chair, usually positioned on the other side of a vast table, can be made easier if the Chairman gets up and comes round the table to welcome and seat the candidate.
- Do smile at the candidates! A pleasant enquiry as to the candidate's journey or accommodation helps to relieve the tension.
- Decide beforehand what kind of interview you are intending to have. It may be that you prefer to hold a more relaxed interview, with all the members of the interviewing team and the candidate sitting in a circle, talking in an unstructured manner about matters that will give a better idea of the candidate's ideas and thoughts on the post and how it should be filled.
- Do not be afraid to try out new ways of conducting appointment interviews. If they don't work, you can try something different, but it is worth experimenting to find out what **does** work.

There are certain matters that the appointing committees must find out at the interview, but it is a waste of time to question a candidate about matters given on the application form, unless you wish the candidate to expand or clarify them. For example, you may wish to know why the candidate was unemployed for a year. Information you need to know is:

- What initiatives the candidate has taken in previous jobs, and what has been achieved, planned and organised.
- What he or she has had published.
- What interests the candidate has outside work, which will tell you whether or not the candidate is a well-rounded person.
- How the candidate sees the post, and how it could be enhanced and/or changed.
- The state of the candidate's health, although you will of course have a medical examination for the successful candidate.
- What the candidate's home circumstances are. How far the candidate would have to travel, or if there would be any difficulty with children at holiday time or when work calls the candidate away.
- What further education the candidate has taken or anticipates taking.
- Where the candidate sees his or her career developing.

Remember that equal opportunities legislation **must** be taken into account at interviews.

1.3 Follow-up to the interview

It is the assessor's duty to see candidates who have not been successful and give them some idea of why their application failed. This feedback should be:

- carried out in private
- as honest as possible.

It should seek to help candidates be successful at any future interviews, so weaknesses must be discussed. It is important that strengths are also discussed and that the candidate sees the exercise as developmental and positive in character.

It may not be appropriate to offer counselling immediately after an unsuccessful interview. The assessor should be sensitive enough to spot this and to offer to write to the candidate, should the candidate wish this, or to speak to the candidate on the telephone at a later date. This kind of counselling should never be pressed on a candidate, who may prefer not to receive it.

The decision of the panel should be communicated to candidates as soon as possible after the interview. If they have not been asked to remain, they should, if possible, be notified by telephone on the same or next day.

2. Being a candidate

At some time or another, almost everyone will be the candidate for a post. We don our best bibs and tuckers and head off for our interview, usually with little preparation. This is a somewhat careless approach as much can be done to increase the odds in our favour by a little preparation.

2.1 Preliminaries

- Ask yourself if this post is **really:**
  - what you want
  - what you are capable of.

  Read the advertisement carefully, particularly the job description.
- If you are not sure, ask for a preliminary visit to see where you will be working and who you will be working with.
- When writing your application form, if you are asked to complete one, send with it:
  - your curriculum vitae (CV)
  - a **short** letter which **does not repeat what you have already said**
  - an explanation of any important matters — for example, why you were not employed for two years — which the employing authority cannot get from your CV or from the application form.
- Make sure that the questions on the form are clearly and succinctly answered. **Type** answers if your handwriting is not clear. **Check the spelling and grammar! KEEP A COPY OF EVERYTHING YOU SEND.**
- Do not be afraid to ask for further information which you may require.

When you are told that you have been shortlisted and are given an interview date, find out as much as you possibly can about the post, the kind of authority you might be working for and any information that will help you to decide to proceed or not, or help you be a better candidate. **Do not try to lobby assessors or members of interviewing panels.**

For references, choose people who will:

- carry some weight with the prospective employers
- know your work and what you are capable of, and know what the post you are applying for entails. If they don't, brief them.

2.2 The interview

On the day of the interview remember:

- The interviewers are **not** monsters. They are often almost as nervous as you, so put them at their ease!
- You may expect to be treated with courtesy and to be given a fair opportunity to express your ideas and feelings.
- You may also expect that the questioning will be searching and possibly

hard. Make sure you have understood every question before you try to answer it. Take your time and think before you reply. Do not talk too much, and answer clearly and audibly. You should expect to be questioned on:

— your education, training and future career aspirations
— your health
— your home circumstances
— your outside interests (hobbies)
— your motivation in applying for the post
— anything that the interviewers may feel impelled to ask! Do not be surprised to be asked what football team you support, even if you are a woman!

Appointment panel members are often unsure as to what they can/should ask, and others are mischievous! If you find any interviewer intimidating, just imagine that he or she is sitting there in the nude. This removes some of the terror, but be careful not to laugh!

You will sometimes find that there is one panel member who wants to find out what you know about current affairs, so it is wise to be aware of things happening in the world. It is also wise to try not to take any 'way out' view of them. You can always say that you have not arrived at any strong opinion as you are waiting to see what transpires. Answer as honestly as you can and do not try to guess what answer the questioner **wants** you to give.

Do not allow yourself to be drawn into political or religious discussions. The evening gathering, when you are invited to meet members of the interviewing panel informally, can be full of pitfalls of this kind.

You will almost inevitably be asked 'Do you have any questions for the panel?' Think out, before hand, what questions you have which are relevant to the post. Questions of salary, amount of leave and so on are not relevant here. You can find these out from the Personnel Department, and perhaps should have done so before applying.

Finally, remember that you have much to give, but you must sell yourself. That is, you must convince the panel that what **you** have to give is of greater value than any of the other candidates.

Hints for candidates

How do members of an interviewing panel arrive at the answers they want from candidates? The answer is, of course, through asking questions. Chapter 2 discussed **open** and **closed** questions and their use. There are also other forms of questions that can be used and prospective candidates may find it useful to consider these, to learn how to recognise what they seek to establish:

(1) Extending questions: These encourage the recipient to pursue a line of thought or to probe more deeply into feelings — 'Could you tell me more about that.'

(2) Clarifying questions: Used when you are not quite sure you understand what is being said — 'I'm not sure of the question. Could you explain it?'

(3) Leading questions: These are the questions, not allowed in court proceedings, which make it quite clear what answer is required — 'I expect you know all about that, don't you?'

(4) Hypothetical questions: These present a hypothetical situation and ask how it might be dealt with — 'Suppose three of your staff told you that they were unhappy in their work, how would you deal with the situation?' Hypothetical questions are of little value. They rarely yield any real information and may not indicate how the situation would be dealt with in a 'for real' situation.

(5) Double-barrelled questions: These can be very confusing as they ask two, or even more, questions at once, leaving a doubt as to which should be answered first or at all — 'What were your main responsibilities in your last post, how did you decide which were priorities and do you now think that you had your priorities right?' When confronted with such a confusing series of questions, it is best to take the first question and answer it fully. Then, if you have forgotten the other questions, ask 'What else was it you asked me?' The questioner has probably forgotten too by that time!

(6) Questions, offering alternatives: 'Would you deal with an unhappy client by disagreeing with him, by arguing with him, by agreeing with him or simply by listening to him?' These are the kind of 'multiple choice' questions which are easy to answer when they are in a written form, but very difficult when presented verbally.

(7) Questions that imply a value judgement: Here the questioner makes it plain what his or her stance is on a particular point, and the question may be an implied criticism of yours — 'What on earth made you do that?'

3. Induction of staff

3.1 Why bother?

The purpose of induction is:

- to systematically introduce the new appointee to the post and its responsibilities
- to ensure that the new appointee knows the policies of the organisation
- to ensure that the new appointee has completed all the personnel and personal aspects of the employment, and is fully aware of terms and conditions of employment
- to provide any training, orientation visits or lectures which will be needed in the new post.

It has been demonstrated that when these matters are competently dealt with in the first weeks of employment, the employee quickly becomes an active and productive member of the organisation and the team. It has also been shown that good induction can reduce wastage. To allow a new employee to stumble around an unfamiliar organisation, and possibly make blunders, is unforgivable and counterproductive. In doing so, the appointee may establish a reputation that is quite unjustified, and may suffer from it for a long time afterwards.

It is also the responsibility of new appointees to ask for an induction programme. Do you remember the question asked at the interview, 'Miss Bloggs, do you have any questions for the panel?' This may be the time to say 'Yes, what is the policy regarding the composition and length of induction programmes?' You may get the answer that that is something for management to decide, but you will have indicated the fact that you are expecting such a programme.

3.2 What kind of induction should it be?

Good induction takes into consideration the following aspects of the appointee's work and life:

- Personal matters such as the reception and acceptance of the contract of employment, handing in P45 and tax forms to the Personnel Department, medical examination, and so on. **Every employee should have a contract of employment.** Every employee should read it carefully and keep it in a safe place.
- The responsibilities of the post **in detail.** What is expected by the manager and the organisation.
- The policies of the organisation. Such policies should be in document form and be handed to the new arrival for perusal at leisure.
- Introduction to the other team members even if they have met before informally, and briefing as to relationships with other teams or professionals. This is usually information readily given. The new appointee will, however, be wise to reserve judgements and make up his or her own mind as to personalities. It is wise to **note** what is said, and to be careful not to make avoidable mistakes.
- Any training or induction meetings which may be required.

3.3 How long should induction take?

This will depend on two main factors:

- how long the appointee **needs** – induction should proceed at the appointee's own pace
- what special training is needed.

If the induction is a lengthy one, there is no reason why, if the manager feels that it is reasonable, the new appointee should not begin to carry out certain tasks even though the induction has not been completed.

No employee should be expected to make any serious contribution to the work until induction is complete.

It is up to the employee to ensure that he or she has all the information needed to enable him or her to do the job properly.

It is the manager's responsibility to provide induction

It is the employee's responsibility to ensure that he or she is capable of doing the job, or to insist on receiving further training.

3.4 Checklist for the induction of a member of staff

The following checklist is meant as a model that could be adapted to suit local needs. It may not be comprehensive. It should also be a guide for new employees to check that they have received adequate induction in their new post.

Following appointment before taking up post

- Letter of confirmation
- Medical examination
- Receipt and signature of contract of employment
- Starting date and joining instructions
- Possible induction programme, although this is sometimes given to new appointees on their first day
- Assistance in finding somewhere to live, if non-resident.

First day in post

Visit to Personnel Department:

- to receive staff handbook
- to learn about Occupational Health Department
- to be shown car parking (if any)
- to be told about:
  - transport facilities
  - residence
  - social facilities, sports facilities, any other facilities
  - safety and fire arrangements
  - where to change, if uniform is worn, and where to leave clothes
  - rules about smoking
  - where the restaurant is and times of meals.

Taken to meet the manager to be told about:

- times of arrival at work
- off-duty arrangements, requests for special off duty
- local safety and fire precautions
- the layout of the ward or office where he or she will work
- colleagues and be introduced to **one** or **two** of them — do not try to introduce everyone on the first day, as the new employee may not remember the names, and that could be held against him or her later
- where and how meals are taken
- where the lavatory is!

Over the first week

- Gradually introduce colleagues, possibly arranging a short meeting with the most important ones.
- Introduce the new employee to meetings, particularly those he or she will need to attend in future, but making it clear that he or she is not expected to contribute anything yet.
- Protect the new employee from the opportunist who will try to get him or her to agree to something, out of ignorance, that has been thrown out of court ten times already!
- Gradually allow the new employee to take over the less difficult parts of the job.

- Ask the new employee, from time to time, if there is anything else that he or she wants to know or do.
- Arrange any visits to other departments, areas or institutions with which the new employee will be liaising or meeting.
- Ensure that the new employee **knows** that your door is open to him or her at any time during the initiation period for help and advice.
- Warn the new employee of any pitfalls to be avoided, any difficult members of staff that need to be handled carefully and any idiosyncrasies of people or systems that need to be known.

After three to six months

The first SD&PR interview should take place after this time. Objectives should be set for the first time, a review of progress made and any further training needs, visits or other developmental requirements catered for.

Suggested further reading

John Courtis, *The 44 Most Common Management Mistakes and How to Avoid Them* (Kogan Page and the British Institute of Management, 1988).

Clive Fletcher, *How to Face the Interview* (Unwin, 1986).

Clive T. Goodworth, *Effective Interviewing for Employment Selection* (London: Business Books, 1983).

Philip Hodgson, *A Practical Guide to Successful Interviewing* McGraw-Hill Book Company, 1987).

Martin John Yate, *Great Answers to Tough Interview Questions* (Kogan Page, 1988).

Chapter 6   Co-ordinating

Introduction

It will be remembered that the sixth main area of managerial tasks was that of co-ordinating. This chapter considers the skills needed for the most efficient and effective presentation of material which the manager wants to get across to listeners. A detailed account of how to make such presentations has been included as most first-line managers, particularly those in the community, will, at some time, be involved in these activities. These skills, some of which are common to all forms of presentations, relate to:

- using equipment (overhead projectors, charts and so on)
- writing reports
- speaking to small groups
- making a speech
- educating the public.

Making an effective presentation

Once again the main prescription for success lies in the **preparation** and the care with which every eventuality is catered for well in advance of the great day! The steps in such preparation will be very familiar to those who have read previous parts of this book, but a repetition will help to emphasise their importance.

1. What are the objectives of making this presentation?

Presentations can be used to extract extra resources from a reluctant management or to show the superiority of **your** demands over those of others. Fighting for scarce resources is an art which these days needs to be well practised. They are also used to show what has been accomplished.

2. Who is the presentation for?

It is vital that you should be aware of your audience, its possible reactions to certain ways of giving information, who will be the allies and who the enemies, and what statistics, or other information, are likely to make most impact. In fact, it is vital to know as much as possible about the audience. Such knowledge will help you offer the most effective presentation, and will prepare you for the difficult or trick question, so it is wise to do your homework.

3. What points do you want to make?

Write down all the points it is important to include. Also list the sticking points, those which may be weak or may not add anything to the argument. You will then need to think very carefully about how you will field questions on these points, so that they do not achieve undue importance and distract attention from the strong points of the argument, or whether to leave them out.

4. How will you do it?

Delivering a 'lecture' or giving a talk are probably the least effective ways of persuading people to do anything, unless you can capture and keep their attention so that your reasoned arguments are heard and listened to with interest and sympathy.

5. What visual aids should you use?

Because it is rare in meetings or presentations of your authority to demonstrate points on an OHP or to use a video, this is no reason why **you** should not do so. People may be somewhat surprised, particularly in rather formal meetings, but remember that impact will capture interest. You may soon find that you have started a whole new fashion in making a case!

6. Making the presentation

- Thank your audience for coming.
- Introduce yourself if you are not known to everyone, and, in any case, tell the audience why **you** are the best person to speak on this particular subject. Have no false modesty!
- If you have taken an expert in some subject (a wise thing to do if you are not absolutely sure of your ground) with you, introduce that person.
- Tell the audience when they can ask questions. Some people like to take questions as they go along, while others prefer to wait until the end. One of the best ways is to say that you will stop from time to time to ask for questions related to the sections of the presentation.
- Open each section by telling the audience what you intend to prove, then go on to prove it, and finally tell them what you have just proved! At the end, summarise the points you have raised and proved, and conclude that because you have proved each point, the case as a whole is proved!
- Finally, remember the good advice which is given to speakers: **stand up, speak up, shut up.** In other words, be visible, audible and credible, and never go on for too long. It is much better to make a few points that will be remembered, than to try and cover a vast number, most of which will be forgotten.

Using equipment

The embarrassment of watching a speaker falling over cables, failing to find the necessary viewfoil, finding that the video does not appear to work, or any of the dozens of things that can go wrong, is so distracting to an audience that any possible impact the speaker could have had is lost. All that anyone will remember will be the apparent, independent life of the equipment which, on that day, seemed hell bent on making an ass of the speaker. The speaker could be excused for a feeling that the equipment had a malevolent determination to get him or her!

In fact, when this happens, there is only one person to blame – the speaker. There are one or two rules which anyone who does not wish to appear a complete idiot would do well to remember:

- Do not depend on technicians to prepare equipment for you.
- Test all equipment carefully before you use it.
- Make sure that the equipment provided will take the material you wish to use.
- Leave nothing to chance – **Check, Check, Check.**

1. Visual aids

1.1 Overhead projector

Watching people talking to groups, it almost seems as though everyone feels that they **must** use the overhead projector (OHP)! The first question to ask, therefore, is 'Do I need it?'

What slides (if any) are needed?

A slide is only needed if it can illustrate what you want to say more effectively than your words can, or if it will reinforce what you are saying. It must, therefore, have **impact.**

Use a slide to demonstrate headings which you will discuss one at a time, but which together make a coherent whole, as illustrated by the following:

```
┌─────────────────────────────────────┐
│                                       │
│   THE TASKS OF MANAGEMENT             │
│                                       │
│   (1) PLANNING                        │
│                                       │
│   (2) ORGANISING                      │
│                                       │
│   (3) STAFFING                        │
│                                       │
│   (4) LEADING                         │
│                                       │
│   (5) CONTROLLING                     │
│                                       │
│   (6) CO—ORDINATING                   │
│                                       │
└─────────────────────────────────────┘
```

In this case, each task can be described and explained while, at the same time, the six tasks are displayed to emphasise their importance and to reinforce what the speaker is saying.

A slide is **not** needed to act as a repeat of what you are saying. For example:

This applies to single words or to whole sentences. Either way, their display is distracting, and adds nothing to the presentation.

How much should be put on each slide?

Not too much. Remember, whatever it is, it must have **impact.** The slide that contains row upon row of words distracts the listener and adds little to the presentation.

Not too little. If, for example, you are talking about public health, there seems little point in putting up a slide which says:

```
┌─────────────────────────────────────┐
│              PUBLIC HEALTH            │
└─────────────────────────────────────┘
```

There might, however, be some use in offering a list of the component parts of public health which you are going to talk about. For example:

```
┌─────────────────────────────────────┐
│                                       │
│   PUBLIC HEALTH                       │
│                                       │
│   (1) WATER                           │
│                                       │
│   (2) SEWAGE                          │
│                                       │
│   (3) HOUSING                         │
│                                       │
│   (4) HEALTH EDUCATION                │
│                                       │
│   (5) PREVENTIVE MEASURES             │
│                                       │
│   (6) COMMUNITY HEALTH PROVISIONS     │
│                                       │
└─────────────────────────────────────┘
```

What can be put on a slide?

- **Colour:** Do use colour if at all possible. Go to your nearest design shop or stationers and look at what they have to offer. There is a wealth of coloured papers, pens and other materials which can cheer up your presentation.
- **Diagrams:** One of the advantages of slides is that diagrams can be traced from drawings which you have made on ordinary paper, or from magazines or books (always clear with authors that such diagrams can be used). Make sure that diagrams are **legible** and can be read from the back of the room or hall, or without the audience standing on its head (see Figure 11)!

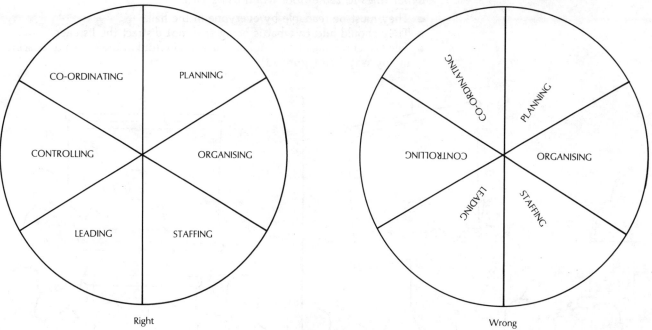

Figure 11 Preparing diagrams for a slide

- **Cartoons and pictures:** You do not need to be an artist to use these, although, if you can find someone artistic who is prepared to draw them for you, it may be helpful. However, anyone can draw 'pin men', or trace useful or amusing line drawings which will illustrate a point you are making.
- **Charts:** Do make sure that they are the best way of demonstrating the information, readable, understandable and relevant (see Figure 12).
- **Tables of figures:** These are to be avoided if possible. They are usually illegible from about the second row of the audience; if they **can** be read, they are distracting and add little, except possibly confusion, to the presentation! Tables of figures are much better offered as 'handouts', if they are needed at all. The speaker can then draw the audience's attention to relevant parts of the charts during the presentation.
- **Technical drawings:** These can be shown, but be careful that they are visible, understandable, add something to the presentation, are simple and can be easily explained by the speaker.

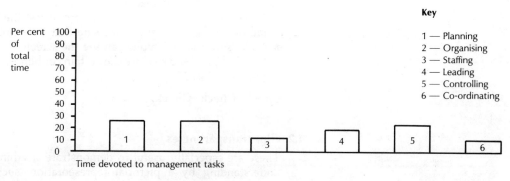

Figure 12 Preparing charts

What not to put on a slide

A failing of many presenters is to insist on putting up slides in hastily scrawled writing which cannot be read, is smudged or even badly spelled! Self-adhesive letters are available to make a more professional slide. If handwriting is preferred, **print** clearly, using ruled lines to make sure that the words are straight. Most OHPs can be used as a form of blackboard, and can be useful used in this way, but even so try to practise good writing.

Other rules to remember when using OHP slides

- They must be readable by everyone in the hall.
- They should **add** to what is being said, **not** distract the listener.
- The presenter must be careful **not** to stand in front of the screen or obscure it in any way (see Figure 13).

Right   Wrong

Figure 13   Positioning a screen

- The slide should never be removed while people are trying to write down what they are being shown. If you do not want them to be distracted in this way, tell them, in advance, that you will provide a 'handout'.
- Check that the slides are in the right order and 'match' the talk you are giving, and that they are numbered, in case you drop them (i.e. are they in the right order?)
- Check that the OHP works! Nothing is worse than finding that you have the wrong plug on the machine, or no plug, or no socket near enough to plug in to.
- Check the focussing **before** you stand up to speak, and make sure you know how that particular machine works.
- Make sure that you have somewhere to rest the slides, so that they will not fall on to the floor, and make sure that your notes are also at hand.
- Make sure that everyone can see the screen.
- Check if you need to close the curtains or blinds, and are there curtains which you **can** close?

Check, Check, Check.

1.2 Film transparencies

These are especially useful to demonstrate anything that lends itself to better understanding by a pictorial representation, such as, for example, clinical conditions.

The notes on the use of OHPs also apply to film transparencies. Some additional points are as follows:

● If the projector is in the middle of the audience, care must be taken to see that the cables are securely anchored, so that people do not fall over them as they go in and out of the hall.
● If the projector is in a projection room, make sure that you have arranged a signal with the projectionist, so that he or she knows when to change the slides.
● Make sure that the slides are loaded the right way up and in the right order. It is easy to put a numbered, coloured spot on each one which will tell you how to load them.

1.3 Use of video

Video has two main uses.

Closed circuit television

Closed circuit television (CCTV) is used to record activities in the training room. When using CCTV, remember that some people may feel threatened by this use of video, so it is wise to bear in mind the following:

● Always **ask** if people wish to take part, and do not use unfair ways of persuading them – for example, by saying 'You aren't afraid, are you? Surely not!'
● Do not play back the recording to large groups if it contains material which could be embarrassing to anyone.
● Ask participants if they are willing for others to see the video.
● A short talk on **feedback,** how to give and receive it, should be given before comments are asked for.
● Encourage sensitive and positive feedback given in the way already described.
● Discourage observers telling participants they were 'Very good!' The acting ability of the participant is not the primary function of using CCTV, nor is it helpful to avoid giving feedback about failings, even in an effort to save the participant's face.
● Discourage sniggering or laughing at what has been said. Even if the participants did say some rather silly things, they will see it all too quickly for themselves, and may be inhibited from taking part again if they feel they have been made to look foolish.
● Demonstrate that you have 'wiped' the recording at the end of the session. Participants usually do not wish such a record to be available for others to see.

The main strength of CCTV is that those who are involved can see themselves as they really are, can identify habits which they did not know they had or can recognise shortcomings in their relationships with others.

Showing video and other films

The second use of video is to demonstrate something, for training or other purposes. When using video for this reason it is important to consider the following points:

● Why are you showing this film? In other words, what are your objectives?
● How will it be shown? It has been said that the attention span of an audience is usually only about 15–20 minutes, which is about the frequency of advertisements on the television. Even when films are shown without breaks, most people find their attention wandering, and it has to be a very gripping film indeed to hold the watcher's attention for longer. Without being aware of it, the watcher's mind strays, returning when it is sufficiently rested. It is wise, therefore, to show only short sections of a film at a time, each section having a specific message. Many videos, particularly those made for teaching purposes, have workbooks which suggest exercises or discussion points to be used with the film. This mix of film, exercises and discussion is a happy combination which lends itself to a productive use of video.
● When will it be shown? The post-prandial use of films, with the participants sitting in the dark, dozing gently after a good lunch or dinner, adds nothing

to their understanding. Show films or videos at a time when people are alert, and give them specific points to watch for.

Using video and films in a productive way will place responsibility on the user to:

- ensure that the video fits the machine (VHS? Betamax?)
- go through the film before showing it, to decide where to stop it to make a point or do an exercise
- go through the film before showing it, to make a note of the numbers shown on the counter at the different sections so that they can be found without difficulty
- make sure that he or she is familiar with the film and prepared for any questions that may arise.

1.4 White and black boards

The main rule for the use of this media is never to use it if you find it difficult to write **clearly, legibly** and in a **straight line** on such a board. Like the 'flip chart', it is useful for making quick notes of what is being said. For example, it is useful when used in brainstorming when the solutions to a problem can be called out by members of the group and written on the black/white board or flip chart.

1.5 Charts, displays and bookstalls

Charts

The use of charts can be invaluable in making a presentation understandable and lively. They can take the form of:

- pie charts (Figure 14a)
- bar charts (Figure 14b)
- columnar charts (Figure 14c)
- curves (Figure 14d)
- dot charts (Figure 14e).

All of these are used to demonstrate comparisons between such things as items, frequencies, components, times or relationships. If used sparingly, and if they are easily understood, they can have a great impact on an audience. They can be shown on slides, transparencies or drawn on large cards to be put into displays, or used to demonstrate points in a presentation. If used as the adjunct to a lecture or demonstration, the user should ask:

- What will they contribute to the whole?
- Is this the most effective way of demonstrating what I want to say?

Displays

Charts, pictures or diagrams can be mounted on walls or stands and placed around a room, at its entrance or where the audience will take food or drink. Such displays add emphasis to the subject matter under discussion, and often show a different perspective, or another dimension of the subject. If they are colourful and interesting, their impact can leave a lasting impression on the audience.

Bookstalls

Local bookshops and specialist bookshops are usually happy to be asked to provide a reasonably comprehensive collection of books on specific subjects. Audiences can then see what literature would contribute to their knowledge of a subject, and can order or buy books, which will please the bookseller!

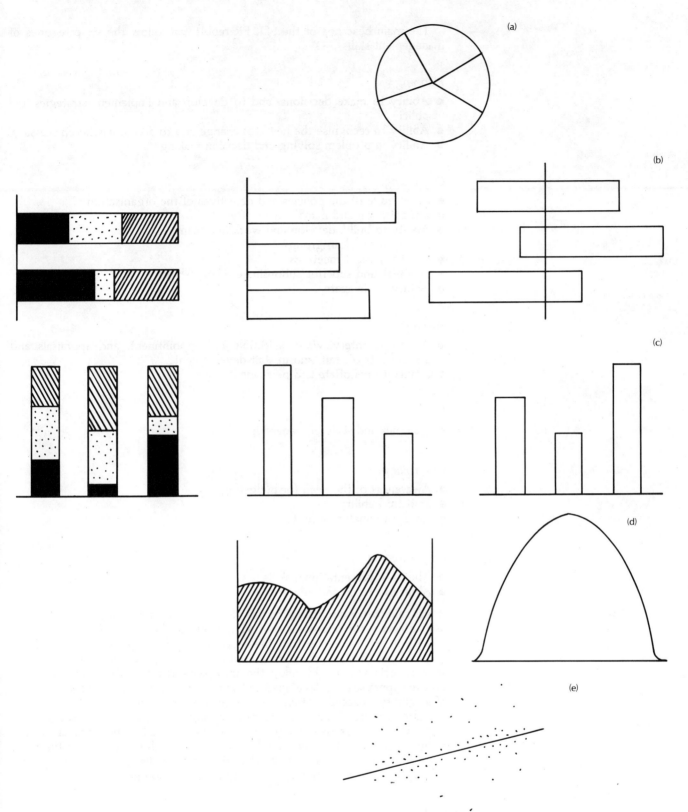

Figure 14 Types of charts

Writing reports

1. What kind of report?

1.1 SD&PR reports, summaries and references

Before embarking on these, it is well to remember that it is the appraisee's career and future which you are writing about, so it is important to be honest and fair, and also to ensure that what is said will acknowledge improvements made. You know the appraisee but others will not, so it is vital that you consider **allowable weaknesses** in the context of the team and refer to strengths that make them acceptable.

The main headings of the SD&PR report can follow the six categories of management skills:

Planning
- Ability to make decisions, and to develop and implement strategies and policies.
- Ability to recognise the need for change and to accept it where necessary.
- Ability in problem solving and decision making.

Organising
- Knowledge of the policies and objectives of the organisation.
- Organisation and management of work.
- Ability to build, develop and work in a team.
- Ability to work in groups.
- Effectiveness at meetings.
- Personal, and superior/subordinate relationships.
- Ability to delegate.

Staffing
- Ability in interviewing, selection and appointment, and appraisals and assessments of staff, and in staff development.
- Ability to negotiate and persuade.

Leading
- Qualities and style of leadership.

Controlling
- Awareness of the need for budgeting.
- Statistical ability.
- Ability to analyse reports.

Co-ordinating
- Ability in presentational skills.
- Ability to teach and educate.

It was said, when discussing the use of SD&PR forms, that they should not be used **directly** for references, but summaries can be made of their contents, which will help to demonstrate the development of the appraisee over a period of time, and they are commonly used for that purpose. Such summaries are short reports and should reflect the appraisee's ability at the time of writing, how the appraisee has developed and, in particular, how this has been the result of an ability to accept criticism and to learn from training.

References are also a form of report writing, linked, as we have seen, to the SD&PR summaries. Most references ask very specific questions about the ability, mentally, physically, intellectually and psychologically, for the post. The referee must be aware of what the post entails, and be sure to give information which will be most useful in the selection process.

1.2 Explanatory reports

Accident reports, for example, require the inclusion of careful and detailed data, which will be of value when making decisions about the action to be taken. Many of these reports are written on special forms, but there is often a place for extra information which may be of value. It is essential to be precise, accurate and detailed.

Incidents that have occurred with patients, clients or relatives can also be described as explanatory reports. They, like accident forms, can become legal documents, and it is wise to remember this when writing them. Wherever possible, the names and addresses of witnesses should be included. With legal action becoming more and more common, it is wise to be very precise in describing incidents and, if at all possible, in obtaining proof of the statements you are making.

1.3 Ward and community nurses' reports

Again these type of reports can become legal documents, possibly of value to either party in a legal action, but if the information is careless or illegible, they will be of little value, possibly when most needed!

Apart from their use for these purposes, they are also a record of the medical progress of a patient or a client and/or his or her needs, and may offer the only clue to other nurses as to what should be done for patient or client. Other professionals may also refer to these notes. Beware of using shortened forms of words, jargon or other expressions which obscure the meaning.

1.4 Making a case, making a proposal and giving information

These will be referred to later.

2. How to write the report

It is wise, when writing reports, to start in note form and to progress to the final form in an ordered series of steps. (This also applies to writing notes for speeches.)

- What is the purpose of the report (and therefore what **must** be included)?
- What information are you going to offer?
  - What has been said about this subject before?
  - What is relevant **now**? Will it achieve the purpose?
  - Does any of the information apply to us?
- Check the accuracy of the information.
- Write the report in rough.
- Does it read logically?
- Put in the headings wanted.
- Put in any diagrams, charts or statistics.
- Assemble it in the best possible manner. Scissors and paste are invaluable if you do not have access to a word processor.
- Write the first 'fair' copy.
- Revise by: reading through and checking for unnecessary sections, words or phrases; taking out any clumsy phrases; improving the English and syntax; ensuring that it is understandable to whoever will read it.
- Ask yourself – If I were reading this, would I want to read it, and would I be convinced?
- When the second rewrite is finished, put it away. Do not continue to tinker! Over editing may mean that you are putting back what you removed at the last edit!
- Number the paragraphs. There is usually a convention for numbering paragraphs which you can discover by looking at other reports. Try to keep to the form of numbering and style commonly used in your authority. It is less confusing for your readers.

3. The form of the report

Most reports are written in the following form:

- The heading, which gives the name of the report, who it is for and why it was commissioned.
- The table of contents.
- The introduction (tell them what you are going to say).
- The main argument (say it).
- The conclusion (tell them what you have said).
- The recommendations.
- The appendices. (Those things which would be of interest but which are not absolutely vital to the report. Some people will read them, some will not.)
- The date of the report and who wrote it.

Certain reports need extra attention to statistics, tables or diagrams. Reports which make a case or a proposal or give information are almost certain to fall into this category. Statistics are notoriously difficult to understand and should be only included if they add something to the text and are understandable to the proverbial child of five! If it is necessary to add long passages explaining the statistics, there seems little point in including them. So, make sure that such aids to persuasion are **relevant, understandable** and **add something to the text.**

Rules on writing reports	(1) Find out what the commissioning agent(s) wants and try to provide it. (2) Keep it short and alive, the sort of report that would make good bedside reading and deprive you of sleep until you had finished it! (3) Check the spelling, English and syntax. If you are not sure, consult an expert. (4) Take out redundant phrases. (5) Write in the third person – 'It should be noted that . . .' – rather than 'I (or we) have noticed that . . .' (6) Check the accuracy of all statements, statistics and data. (7) Make sure it reads logically. (8) Make sure the conclusions and recommendations are clear. They will, in all probability, be the only parts people will read! (9) Summaries and extrapolations from long reports are often asked for, and are useful to emphasise the main points.

Making a speech

Many of us are reduced to quivering jellies when faced with the prospect of speaking in public. Nursing, with its element of preventive medicine, which makes educating the public a part of the job, places on nurse managers the responsibility of speaking to a wide variety of audiences. The least we can do is to make such careful preparations that our stress level can be controlled. At best we may even come to enjoy public speaking!

1. Know your audience

It has been said that 'An audience is not a ravening, blood hungry beast, nor is it a field of cabbages.' Equally it would be foolish to speak to a group of school children in the same way as you would speak to a group of senior nurses. So thought must be given to:

- the level of intelligence of the audience
- the level of understanding of the subject by the audience
- what jargon or medical terminology they will understand
- what terms or words they use to describe parts of the body, for example
- the degree of interest which they will have. (Some may have been 'sent' and see it as a golden opportunity for a short snooze! You may then have to work very hard.)

2. Make careful preparations

These will follow the kind of preparations which were a prelude to writing a report:

- Setting your objectives.
- Making a plan.
- Deciding on which visual aids to use, if you decide to use them.
- Preparing your notes or script.

The preparation of notes will need some thought. If you know your subject really well, you will need little in the way of written material to keep you on course. The fewer notes you lumber yourself with the better, but it is wise to have some sort of map of what you want to say in the form of notes. Make sure that they are easily readable and that they are attached to each other, so that they do not go flying around the room with yourself in hot pursuit.

Having taken the trouble to write notes, **keep to them.** It is easy to become so carried away with your own rhetoric that you lose touch with time and reasoned argument.

Notes should be a series of headings with key words or phrases which will carry you from one point to the next. There are times when more extensive notes may be necessary but, even so, headings, clearly underlined, will be helpful.

3. On the day

Remember the advice you were given about making presentations.

- Make sure that the microphone works, if you are going to use one.
- Find out where you can put your notes, and decide where you are going to stand. Do not be forced into speaking from a position in which you are uncomfortable.
- Try not to 'wander'. Nothing is more trying to an audience than having to track a speaker like spectators at a tennis match.
- Jokes can enliven a speech, but do make sure that they are appropriate to the audience and fit the point you are trying to make.
- Begin well, by getting the audience 'on your side'. For example, you might tell them that you hope they are not as nervous as you are, or that you know the subject matter is a bit dry, but you will try to make it as interesting as possible.
- Let the audience in on your objectives. Tell them what you hope to achieve and, if you are sure you have achieved it, ask the audience if they agree.
- Questions can be difficult. Before you start, make it clear whether you wish to take questions and when.
- Difficult listeners who try to heckle you from the floor love it if they can get you to take issue with them. **Do not be drawn!** Ask the audience 'What do you think about that?' and if possible let them deal with the heckler. Do distinguish between hecklers and those who have a legitimate but possibly controversial question.
- Breathe deeply before you enter, and make sure you are as calm as you can be. Make a slow, deliberate entrance. Put down your notes and arrange your visual aids. Look round the audience with a pleasant smile. Take another deep breath. Introduce yourself (if no one else has done it). Do not begin until you are quite ready.
- Do not fidget or walk about, and beware of the 'er ... um ... you knows'.
- Try to inject sincerity and interest into your voice. If **you** are interested, your audience will be too. Do not fix any one poor creature with your eye, but let your gaze wander over the whole audience so that they will feel that they are all included.
- Try and end with a comment that will send the audience away with something that will stick in their minds. For example, if you have been speaking to a group of nurses about management, you might say 'I have shown you how poor management can lead to costly mistakes. When you return to work tomorrow, you might ask yourselves, what am **I** doing which could do the same to **my** authority?'
- Finally, practise on small groups and work your way up, read other people's speeches and listen to others, noting their mistakes as well as their successes.

Suggested further reading

Trevor J. Bentley, *Report Writing in Business* (Kogan Paul and CIMA, 1987).

Clive Fletcher, *How to Face the Interview* (Unwin, 1986).

Clive T. Goodworth, *Effective Interviewing for Employment Selection* (Business Books, 1979).

Clive T. Goodworth, *Effective Speaking and Presentation for the Company Executive* (Business Books, 1980).

Philip Hodgson, *A Practical Guide to Successful Interviewing* (McGraw-Hill, 1987).

Greville Janner, *Janner's Complete Speechmaker* (Business Books, 1984).

Greville Janner, *On Presentation* (Business Books, 1984).

Antony Jay, *Slide Rules* (Visual Arts, 1986).

Antony Jay, *Effective Presentation* (British Institute of Management (BIM), 1985).

A. G. Mears, *The Right Way to Speak in Public* (Cox & Wyman, 1978).

Simon Mort, *How to Write a Successful Report* (Business Books, 1983).

L. S. Powell, *A Guide to the Use of Visual Aids* (British Association for Commercial and Industrial Education (BACIE), 1981).

L. S. Powell, *A Guide to the Overhead Projector* (BACIE, 1980).

Chris Waller, *Using Your Overhead Projector and Other Visual Aids* (Fordigraph Division of Ofrex, 1983).

Martin John Yate, *Great Answers to Tough Interview Questions* (Guildford: Biddles Ltd., 1988).

Gene Zelazny, *Choosing and Using Charts* (Video Arts, 1972).

The Way to Better Presentations (SASCO Ltd.).

Report Writing (BACIE, 1981).

Tips on Talking (BACIE, 1983).

Part III

Practical Applications of Communications

Part III of this book considers the areas of nurse management at the point of delivery of care and the specific communication needs of special groups of patients or clients.

Chapter 7

Communication in nurse management at the point of service delivery

Introduction

In 1981 an important book entitled *Communication in Nursing Care*[1] was published. It was edited by Will Bridge and Jill Macleod Clark and the contributors were nursing academics and researchers. In the Foreword, Phyllis Friend, then Chief Nursing Officer at the DHSS, said 'The dominant theme of the book is that communication is not an optional extra in nursing care, but a central feature of the role of the nurse. Hospital wards where communication is effective are not simply more pleasant places to be in; this book shows that they are also places in which patients recover more quickly, and suffer less pain and anxiety.'

Since that time the English National Board, in its newly designed syllabus, has shown how much importance it attaches to good communication and the role that experiential training can take in showing the learner, trained and untrained, that communication is the central pivot of the therapeutic community where all other nursing skills rest.

Throughout this book better ways of communicating have been suggested. It must be said that many competent nurse managers have inter-personal skills that they have developed to a high degree of efficiency without any training. It must also be said that there are many who return from training courses with a strong sense of the need to change their practices, and find that the climate to which they return makes that an impossibility. Moreover, in the rough and tumble of patient and client care, it is easy to forget to use even those skills which have been recognised as central to good care, and few of us are able to be constantly aware of their use when good intentions become swamped by pressure and stress, or lost in concentration on accurate and safe procedures. The only way to improve one's communication skills is to know intellectually what **should be** and to practise the skills until they become second nature in their use.

To examine further the question of the central role of communication in nurse management, we must first ask how nurses see themselves. From observation and research it would appear that they view their main role and function as providers of treatment, advice and care. The management element of their role is often ignored, poorly understood and sometimes denied. Yet the management element of nursing at this level, if translated into industrial or business terms, would be considered as supporting a high degree of responsibility and accountability, and would place them in a higher category than that of mere supervisors.

It cannot be repeated often enough that **all** efficient and effective management has its roots in skilled communication. This chapter will consider the areas of nurse management at the point of delivery of care for **all** nurses, both trained and untrained, and differences, where they exist, will be mentioned. These differences exist as a result of the various grades, the different tasks that they perform and by the differing skills implicit in the varied levels of training and ability.

The main management areas are:

- the management of **time** and **work**
- the management of **teams, groups** and **individuals**
- the management of the **quality of the environment**
- the management of **other professionals, other disciplines within their own profession** and **other workers**

- the management of **patients** or **clients**
- the management of **relatives** of patients or clients
- the management of **budgets** (which, as before, will not be discussed, but the reader is referred to another book in the series, *Managing Finance*).

Managing time and work

At ward level, and in the community nursing service, there are certain constraints that must be met at certain times of the day, or on set days of the week; there are also constraints of time which are thought to be immutable and around which all other events are arranged. Of some, this is true, of others it may be questionable.

Within certain limits, these constraints for most wards or community 'patches' are constant throughout the country, and the culture of the nursing profession has, to some extent, encouraged this standardisation of procedures, which has had a number of effects:

- It has ensured that nurses are familiar with the overall routine of most wards or community areas within their hospital or district and, as a result, could probably function at a reasonable level of proficiency in most comparable areas of the country.
- It means that moving from ward to ward, in the formative training years, is for the learner, less traumatic, as all the trainee has to consider is 'Sister's little ways', minor matters of routine or things that are 'not done here!'
- It enables nurse teachers, and those whose business it is to set and maintain standards, to do so more effectively and easily.
- It may mean that familiarity leads to the acceptance of a *status quo* which, if examined critically, might not be supportable by rational considerations.

The conclusions that can be drawn from these comments is that much more time, at local and national level, must be given to thinking about the management of time, and to the possibility that **some** sacred cows could be quietly slaughtered! What must not be sacrificed are the advantages of conformity on the altar of progress and in the name of modern management theory.

Certain theories about nursing also seem to be universally accepted. For example, it is almost universally accepted that nurses are overworked and that in some places there is a permanent shortage of staff. Some of these theories may hold water, but it is important to keep them constantly under review, to examine the way in which tasks are performed and to consider whether some tasks are really necessary. This can be best done by looking at what we are **trying** to achieve and what, in fact, we **do** achieve.

It is part of the first-line manager's job to look critically at these matters, to create a slot in each working week for creative thinking. The time-honoured custom of a bustling, active and task-oriented approach to work, which starts at the moment we enter the ward or drive up to the home of a client, must be balanced by giving time to the planning and the appraisal of:

- what **must** be done
- what **should** be done
- what it would be nice to do if only we had the time.

One way of doing this is by an audit of the ward or district which critically examines each management task and seeks the answer to the following questions:

- **Must** this task be done?
- Can it be done in any other way? More effectively or economically?
- If it is not done, what will be lost?
- What other things ought to be done?

Done as a team exercise, spending, for example, one hour each week until the task is completed, this can show up the areas of work which are taken for granted but which could be either discarded or changed, and can demonstrate how communications take place in that team, and how every member can contribute if given the opportunity.

Time and work should be under constant discussion, consideration and, where necessary, adjustment to take in the changing needs of a ward or district. It is the task of first-line managers to **direct** this exercise, and of **all** nurses to be aware of it.

Time is a unique resource. It cannot be bought, sold or stored up, yet it is the one resource, more than any other, which is commonly used as an excuse for poor communications. Its proper use entails its measurement, an examination of **how** it is used and its management. If we do not know these things we must somehow come to find them out. It is expected that nurses are always busy and rushing about. It is not part of our culture to give much time or thought to what we are really accomplishing, nor are we, as a general rule, aware whether we have achieved the right balance between the quality and the quantity of work done.

Case 1

Some of the nurses were giving out lunches. One elderly gentleman looked eagerly at his lunch and picked up his knife and fork. At that moment a nurse came bustling up and, moving his bed table bearing the lunch well out of reach, popped a thermometer in his mouth.

'What did you do that for?' mumbled the old man. The nurse laughed and patted him playfully on his shoulder.

'I'm putting it out of temptation's way,' she said, 'you haven't had your temperature taken yet!'

In this ward, meal times are seen as secondary to other matters – to everyone except the patients. How might this situation be improved?

---

1. Analysing the use of time

There are three main elements in the use of time.

1.1 Key tasks

Key tasks are those that come under the heading of **'must be done'.** They are so well known and accepted that they are usually regarded as immovable and immutable, and how or when they are done is rarely questioned.

The first part of an audit looks at each task performed by each member of staff on one day. The tasks are noted under the following headings:

Date	Activity	Time begun	Time ended

Alternatively a data sheet could be kept which notes what is being done at each quarter of an hour throughout one day and comments on the importance of each, as follows:

Time	Activity	Comments
8.00		
8.15		
8.30		
8.45		

Having completed the exercise, the activities should be looked at and analysed using the criteria:

● How necessary was the activity?

- Who was the right person to carry it out?
- Who did carry it out?
- Could it have been done more efficiently?
- Could it have been done in a shorter time?
- Which tasks could have been left undone? Delegated?

1.2 Key contacts

Key contacts consist of:

- those who report to you
- those who you report to
- those who give you instructions
- those you give instructions to
- other professionals with whom you interact in some way
- significant others, such as patients, clients and relatives.

Having clarified **who** the contacts are, the time spent with each one is also analysed under the headings:

Date	Purpose of interaction	Time taken

Following the analysis the criteria to use in this case are:

- Are those contacts made because they **need** to be made or because they are pleasant?
- How does each contact help to achieve the objectives of the organisation and the personal objectives of the manager?
- Who is **not** involved who might help achieve these objectives?

1.3 Key skills

Key skills have already been discussed under the elements of management. An audit of their use can be carried out by looking at what was happening under the headings:

Date	Skill used	Time involved

There is no doubt that these exercises are very time consuming, and, as they should be done on days when the ward or district is reasonably busy, they may be better done by researchers rather than by the staff of the ward. The co-operation of senior management will be needed to do this, and the advantage that they will see in such exercises is the excellent information that will be gained about what is happening and where changes could profitably be made. It could be argued that we cannot afford **not** to spend time on analysing and managing time to better advantage, even if **not** done in the way suggested.

Managing human resources

Man management differs from the management of other resources because people, unlike other resources, are **aware** of how they are being treated. At the point of delivery of service there are several areas where it is of particular importance to ensure that man management is well and sensitively dealt with:

- A problem-solving approach to planning and decision making, involving team members and ensuring participation.
- In the area of SD&PR, the approach should be to deal with these matters through joint problem solving, which will produce active participation.
- The third area involves first-line managers with their staff in the rather difficult sphere of discipline. Implicit in the effective management of the human resource is the concept of certain parameters of behaviour which are acceptable to the culture of the organisation. Placed alongside this concept is that of the two-way interaction of positive, dynamic management, which implies an exchange rather than a one-way pattern of instruction and monitoring (see section on 'Quality circles', page 93).
  - People, **all** people, make mistakes.
  - Mistakes, especially in nursing, where they can cause pain or more serious injury, must be pointed out and corrected.

  The reconciliation of these two statements requires consideration, not of **whether** it should be done, but of **how.**

Exercise 17

A learner nurse has come to you, as the trained nurse in charge of the ward, and has told you that he or she has accidentally given twice the dose of a prescribed drug to a patient. It is not likely to be fatal, but it has made the patient feel very ill. The patient has been vomiting, is exhausted and is feeling very anxious.

(1) Enumerate the steps to be taken in dealing with this situation.
    (a) How far would you involve other members of staff, and which ones?
    (b) How would you report such an incident?
(2) Role play an interview where the nurse in charge is very angry and storms at the student, giving the student no opportunity to say much.
    (a) Observers – note the learner's reaction and discuss.
    (b) Brainstorm – how do you think the learner feels? What do you think the learner might do as a result of the interview?
(3) Role play an interview where the nurse in charge takes into consideration:
    (a) How the nurse feels.
    (b) The possible reasons why the nurse made such a mistake.
    (c) How the nurse feels he or she could be helped to avoid such a mistake in the future.
    (d) Discuss what you think the nurse's reactions would be to an interactive, problem-solving approach such as this.
    (e) How do you think the nurse feels now?
(4) Compare the two approaches.

During this exercise, remember:
- The patient must be dealt with first, but it would be unhelpful to leave the nurse in suspense. How could you reconcile the two calls on your immediate attention?
- Whatever **you** may say to the nurse is likely to be less critical that what he or she is saying to him or herself.
- You are seeking **reasons, not excuses.**

Exercise 18

It is not only mistakes that must be dealt with, but also questions of:

- poor personal relationships
- poor time keeping
- careless work
- poor personal appearance, habits or hygiene.

Consider each of these problem areas and discuss how you would deal with each one.

- The fourth area is that of support for other members of staff.

Exercise 19

A young man of 18 has been brought in following a motor bike accident. He has come to the ward straight from theatre and recovery room, and the nursing staff have not seen him before. It will be your duty to tell his parents and his girl friend that he has had to have both legs amputated. You realise that this is going to be a very traumatic time for all members of the staff and for yourself.

(1) How will you deal with it personally?
(2) How will you help your staff to deal with it?

(3) Would you consider offering the young houseman or the physiotherapist an opportunity to discuss it personally with you or as a part of the team?

(4) How might you use the situation to show other nurses how to help the young man and his relatives come to terms with the situation?

(5) Can you identify the stages in the process of grief for such a loss?

Exercise 20

A learner nurse is about to give last offices to a patient. This is the first time that this nurse has seen a dead person – and the nurse is, understandably, upset and apprehensive. You realise that the nurse should try to get over this hurdle as soon as possible. Discuss how you would help the nurse do this.

---

1. Loss of a part of the body

The loss of any part of the body changes the body image that each person has of him or herself, and entails grieving by the loser. Such grieving must be permitted and assisted if a good resolution is to be achieved. There are a number of stages that such people pass through:

- **Denial:** This often means that the person refuses to believe that anything has happened. For example, a refusal by the young man in Exercise 19 to believe that he really has lost both legs. This can be made worse in his case by the 'phantom limb' syndrome.
- **Anger:** This may be against the staff, 'Why did you do that to me. It wasn't necessary. You could have saved my legs.' Or it may be against himself, 'Why did I go out on a wet night with a new bike. What a fool I am.'
- **Depression and fear:** 'No one will want me now. How am I going to manage?' Along with depression often comes an inability to eat or sleep properly. Depression can be so intense that suicidal thoughts can be discerned. Nurses should be prepared for them, for the force of grief, anger or fear, and for the irrational behaviour that they may meet with.
- **Acceptance:** The patient begins to adapt to disfigurement and to realise that there are compensations in most situations. The speed with which the patient will reach the stage of acceptance will depend on the support and help of those around. Not all people will ever reach acceptance. Many will embitter their whole lives by a failure to come to this resolution. Furthermore, anger, depression and fear may return from time to time, to continue to depress the patient. It is interesting to note that in some cultures the amputated limb is ceremoniously buried, in the belief that at the time of death the body will once again become whole. Also, it is not unknown for a patient to dwell on where the lost limb is and to ask as to its disposal.

Managing teams, groups and individuals

The formation, leadership and control of groups and teams has already been discussed in Chapter 4. It would be useful to re-read that section of the book before going further.

Teams in a hospital or community can be uni-disciplinary, multi-disciplinary or multi-professional. They can meet formally or informally.

Formal meetings of teams are usually arranged to look at organisational policy and planning. They are rarely problem solving in character, although they would claim that one of their functions is that of solving problems! However, it has been observed that many problems are solved outside the committee room, usually by the strongest group or the group that can generate most decibels! Such groups usually succeed in getting their solution accepted, but this can only happen if disinterest by other groups allows it. A determined and well-prepared presentation can often persuade a team to change its policies.

Nurses are often too afraid, too apathetic, too tired or too busy to give time to preparing good and effective presentations, and many of the policies foisted upon them are unwelcome, of dubious value, and, had the nurses been more prepared, could have been avoided or changed.

Informal meetings often occur between disciplines within a profession. For example, it would be rare for **all** surgical ward sisters, theatre sisters, anaesthetic sisters, infection control sisters and recovery room sisters to meet formally, although they might have common problems that could be solved were they to do so. What would be much more usual would be for a grouping of nurses with these interests to form at meal breaks, to discuss problems and seek solutions. Mutual respect and a common wish to ensure the smooth running of the service motivate nurses to try to overcome uninformed or unreasonable requests by others.

Groups and teams can be used for a variety of purposes.

1. Group problem solving

The technique of brainstorming has already been described (see Chapter 4). It is a powerful device for taking a fresh look at problems and solving them, but the pattern of team meetings at ward level is usually structured so that the senior person present instructs the other team members rather than consults with them. Opinions **may** be sought, but the culture rarely welcomes a diametrically opposed view, and the value of debate vanishes under the weight of discipline. Thus the junior nurse learner, who may have some fresh and interesting ideas, may only be listened to with scant respect, and the freedom to propose new approaches to old problems is lost in the certainty of the trained staff that 'it has always been done like that, it wouldn't work here.'

University students are taught to question. Nurses are taught to obey. The necessity to act quickly and automatically in the face of crises must not be lost, but the bright, thinking youngster must be encouraged to offer ideas and to try these out, in safety.

Groups that involve all their members in helping to resolve problems gain, not only from the fresh perceptions and solutions offered, but also from the strength that is brought about when every member feels valued and involved (see section on 'Quality circles', page 93).

2. Group teaching and learning

One of the most valued and important parts of the nurses' day can be the afternoon handover, which the profession has fought hard to preserve. It would be interesting to know, however, how many nurses have clarified what they are seeking to achieve at this time. That is, what are the objectives?

- To discuss the diagnosis and treatment of each patient?
- To discuss the progress of each patient?
- To pass on instructions for nursing and medical care?
- To instruct learners in the epidemiology and treatment of disease **in a practical setting,** by observing a patient in the ward?
- All of these?

The manner in which this part of the day is handled varies from place to place, and in some places it has sadly been abandoned because it is seen as being too costly in terms of 'wasted' time.

At its **least** helpful, it is an exercise when the person in charge of the ward reviews the patients, their treatment and progress, and gives instructions as to any changes. The rest of the team listen attentively, occasionally remark on some facet that has been missed and, in some cases, jot down notes on scraps of paper or in small note books. This latter habit may give some nurses the confidence that they will not forget anything, but it seems unnecessary when instructions are already recorded. This form of group learning seems a very negative and unproductive way of passing information. Problem solving does not take place, as problems are discussed only between the trained members of the staff.

At its **best,** this time, in addition to considering changes in the treatment of patients, is also used to discuss the care and treatment of a condition, based on one patient within the ward. This form of group learning could be extended to include discussions of nursing-specific topics, such as ethics, confidentiality or the law, or it could consider developments taking place in the fields of medicine and nursing.

Group leaders owe it to their teams to be well informed and senior managers to ensure that their staff are given the opportunity to be aware of significant writings and developments in the profession. Although it is the team leader who will be the teacher, tutors and/or clinical instructors should be present by invitation from time to time, to contribute from their special expertise. It would also be useful to ask other professional colleagues to take part in these meetings occasionally. Such inputs would be valuable both from the point of view of information gained and also because of the advantage that such contacts would offer in helping the participants to appreciate each others' work and problems.

It is not easy to devise a programme of this type. It would be the responsibility of the team leader to make the arrangements and to ensure strict time keeping. Discussions could be taped and shared with other wards, care being taken to avoid naming patients.

Specimen programme for group teaching

A specimen programme is suggested below where 2–2.30 pm is reserved for a discussion of significant changes in treatment or instructions of individual ward patients, and 2.30–3 pm is used for teaching or discussion. Each nurse should be aware of the week's programme and be prepared to contribute questions or to discuss something that has been read or heard which would be of interest to the group.

- Monday 2.30–3 pm – Case study given by a learner of a ward patient of whom he or she has had prime care during the week. Comments by others on care and treatment.
- Tuesday 2.30–3 pm – Discussion on topic of learner's choice.
- Wednesday 2.30–3 pm – Short talk by Sister or Charge Nurse, or a problem-solving exercise with the group.
- Thursday 2.30–3 pm – Presentation by tutor or clinical instructor based on a patient in the ward, or an issue in nursing.
- Friday 2.30–3 pm – Presentation by a houseman, physiotherapist, radiographer, social worker, chaplain, head porter or other professional on either a patient's case or a hospital issue.
- Saturday and Sunday 2.30–3 pm – Review of the week's changes and discussion of the planned programme for the following week.

Managing the quality of the environment

Quality assurance, quality control and quality circles are issues of great importance in the NHS today where quality of service must not be sacrificed at the altar of value for money, important as this may be. These terms sit more easily in manufacturing industries than in a service 'industry' such as the NHS, but manufacturing industry has much to teach us about the calamities that can occur when the standard of quality is not set and assured.

The first step, which rests with top management, is the resolution of policy issues to ensure that quality levels meet consumer demand. Having determined the policy, every level of management and the 'coal face workers' (CFWs) are involved in its implementation.

British Standards (BS 4778) defines quality as 'The totality of features and characteristics of a product or service that bear on its ability to satisfy a given need.'

BS 4778 defines quality assurance as 'All activities and functions concerned with the attainment of quality.'

BS 4778 defines quality control as 'The aspect of quality assurance which concerns the practical means of securing product or service quality as set out in the specification.'

Management must support the achievement of adequate quality in line with the policy determined by top management and by a total commitment to the philosophy of quality control. The approach must be proactive and preventative in character, and ensure that the service given will be 'right' first time, by the allocation of sufficient resources. This is in contrast to the reactive/detective approach which waits for an unsatisfactory service to be identified by complaint, or identifies it by inspection and assessment and, hopefully, leads to ultimate correction.

1. Quality circles

This aspect of quality control was developed in the 1960s in Japan, and it is said that by the 1980s over one million such circles existed there. In this country, industry first became interested as a result of the phenomenal success of Japanese business enterprises, and it was subsequently introduced into a number of British companies with some success. The system has recently been introduced into the NHS.

Middle and first-line managers co-operate to develop a quality circle composed of between 5–20 employees of all disciplines and professions who have a common interest. The group meets regularly to choose a problem related to the quality of the service provided. The reasons for and the extent of the problem are analysed and possible solutions, which can be tested and validated, are discussed.

Involving the workforce in this way has a number of 'payoffs':

- It makes the workforce more aware of their responsibilities for the provision of a service that meets the standards set by the National NHS policy and the policy of the local Health Authority.
- It reduces the problems of inter-departmental competition, friction and exclusivity, and makes every member of the circle aware of the problems of the others.
- It involves the workforce in identifying and implementing problem solutions, thus ensuring that they will all be committed to its success.

The basic philosophy is to establish control of quality in the CFWs fully backed by management at all levels, rather than in a dependence on inspection or supervision, although these remain as a safety net.

Managing other professionals, other disciplines in nursing and other workers

It must be said that, in the comprehensive sense of the word, other professionals and workers in the NHS are not managed by nurses, who only manage other nurses. However, nurses **do** carry out management tasks when dealing with a number of other professionals and workers. In such cases, nurses **must** maintain good record-keeping systems of information to be shared between professionals, particularly in areas such as child abuse.

1. Within a ward

Within a ward the nurse manager will be responsible for the following:

- Giving instructions to a number of service givers.
- Checking that instructions have been carried out satisfactorily, and monitoring the work of such staff as ward cleaners, orderlies and ward clerks. Where the work is not to the required standard the correct approach is first to point out this failure to the worker. If no improvement occurs, the nurse's immediate superior – in this case the Nursing Officer – is then responsible for an approach to the superior officer of the worker concerned.
- Co-ordinating the visits of other professionals and technicians to the ward so that they do not interfere with each other's work. It is the nurse manager's responsibility to ensure that new members of staff of all kinds are aware of the times at which certain visits are made to the ward, and to arrange appropriate times for the new member of staff to visit. However difficult it may appear, it is the nurse manager's responsibility to ensure that individual patients are not visited by an over-tiring succession of workers. Negotiations can be entered into with most workers and professionals to ensure the best treatment for the patient. The nurse manager has a right to insist on the courtesy of being asked if a patient can be visited, and to refuse such a visit if such a refusal is seen to be in the best interests of the patient.
- Maintaining contact with community medical and nursing personnel so that continuity of treatment can be ensured. This management task is the one most easily neglected by both hospital and community nurses. It is not easy to remember, or to find time, to maintain such a link, but that is no excuse for neglecting such a vital part of the nurse manager's managerial skills. One way of doing this would be to offer an open invitation to community staff, giving a set time on one day of each week when they could visit the ward to

see their own patients and, more importantly, to talk to ward staff. This might well be during one of the 'hand-over' periods each week and the community staff could be offered an opportunity to discuss their job and their problems with ward staff. This facility could be reciprocated by the community staff. Good, strong links between the hospital and the community must be encouraged and maintained if patients are to be discharged from hospital to a prepared and suitable environment at home. They are also invaluable in giving hospital nurses the opportunity to learn something of their patients' lifestyles before they are admitted, and how they can best help them.

Exercise 21

(1) Keep a list of all the service providers who visit the ward or the patient's home during a period of one week. This should be collated under the following headings:

Date	Time of arrival	Time of departure	Purpose of visit

The co-operation of senior management, to provide a researcher to carry out this task, would relieve the front-line manager from this added burden, which may not be undertaken in the first place as it is felt to be too time consuming. It would be of even greater value to seek the co-operation of those who make the visits. Were they to be consulted and involved in research of this kind, they would undoubtedly help by recording their arrivals and departures themselves. Such co-operation would also help them to understand the need and importance of analysing what happens at the workplace, and how it can be made more effective.

(2) When the list is complete, compile a chart, analysing the busiest times.
(3) Consider:
   (a) Would it be better to negotiate a re-arrangement of some of these times to ensure a better spread of visits?
   (b) If it would seem to be desirable to do this, how might you go about it? If the people concerned have been involved in helping to set up and run the exercise, they will wish to know of its outcome, and will be more prepared to assist in any re-organisation.

---

2. Within the community

Recent research has shown that, out of 376 inputs by Health Visitors during a five-day period, the inputs were[2]:

- 154–41% – advising (most of this was concerned with teaching and educating clients)
- 75–20% – supporting clients
- 58–15% – monitoring provision of services or progress of clients
- 58–15% – liaising with other professionals, services or groups
- 18–5% – referring clients
- 13–4% – teaching or instructing students or other community workers.

As in the ward, Health Visitors and District Nurses ensure that clients in their homes receive the services they need and to which they are entitled, and they protect the client from over visiting by a proliferation of service providers.

The management of other staff is similarly associated with giving instructions to service providers as to what is needed by clients, monitoring that the work has been done, checking that it has been done properly and co-ordinating the work of other professionals, a task that nurses, as regular visitors, are in the best position to carry out.

Managing patients or clients

The clinical management of patients or clients is a partnership between doctors and nurses. Nurses manage the nursing care of the patient on an equal professional footing with their medical colleagues, who oversee the overall treatment of the patient. Within certain parameters, nurses also manage the administration of the treatment prescribed by the doctor.

Hospitals in particular have become institutions bound by tradition and custom. Although there may be radical changes in the medical and nursing treatment of patients over a period of time, some traditions become so much a part of the mores of the institution that their purpose or value is no longer considered. 'We've always done it like that' becomes an unconscious basis for much of the routine. Florence Nightingale, were she to return, may marvel over antibiotics and transplants, but she would not be too unfamiliar with the routine of the ward. This is perhaps the strength and the weakness of nursing. While traditional ways of working offer stability, it would certainly be of value to examine, more critically than we do at present, everything that happens in the clinical sphere of the patient, and thereby to determine the rationale of what goes on there. Such analyses should be continuous, and the good nurse manager will constantly ask 'Are we doing unnecessary things?'

Within a ward a nurse manager will be responsible for the management of the patient so that he or she can:

- be prepared to receive patients and balance admissions to conform with the ability of ward staff to care adequately for them – this may involve questioning the admission of patients if, in his or her opinion, the staffing level means that their proper care will be impossible, or lead to dangerous levels of supervision.
- ensure that the patients are given every opportunity to discuss their problems with medical and/or nursing staff
- ensure that information given to patients by medical and/or nursing staff is properly understood
- ensure that treatments and care are given on time and are integrated with other procedures so that the patient receives them at unstressful and reasonable points within the day
- ensure that the patient is discharged to a suitable place of residence
- ensure that the patient has sufficient drugs to take home
- liaise with community staff to maintain continuity of care.

Managing relatives of patients or clients

Relatives have very special needs which the nurse manager must find ways of dealing with. These come within the areas of:

- ensuring that relatives are given the opportunity to meet and discuss their problems with doctors and/or nurses
- ensuring that they understand what they have been told – in this context it must be remembered that both patients and relatives may need to be told 'bad' news several times before they can really take it in, and nurses must be ready to repeat the same things several times over without becoming impatient
- ensuring that, if relatives have to cope with a difficult situation, they can do so or are supported to enable them to do so
- ensuring that they are not left to struggle with transport or other difficulties without support
- ensuring that they are aware of the social service provisions that exist to help those in need
- liaising with local authorities to provide for special needs of patients, clients or relatives.

References

1. Will Bridge and Jill MacLeod Clark, eds., *Communications in Nursing Care* (London: HM + M, 1981).
2. The Health Visitors Association, *Health Visiting and School Nursing Reviewed* (1987).

Suggested further reading

R. Caplan, *A Practical Approach to Quality Control* (Business Books, 1971).

June Clark, *What Do Health Visitors Do?* (Royal College of Nursing, 1981).

David Hallows, *Managing Finance* (Macmillan Education, in the press).

Terry Hill, *Production/Operations Management* (Prentice Hall International, 1983).

Jennifer M. Hunt and Diane J. Marks-Maran, *Nursing Care Plans — The Nursing Process at Work* (HM + M Nursing Publication, John Wiley & Sons, 1986).

Susan Pembrey, *The Ward Sister, Key to Nursing* (Royal College of Nursing, 1980).

Margaret Schurr, *Nurses and Management* (English Universities Press Ltd., 1975).

Chapter 8   Communication in nurse management in different areas of medical care

Introduction

In Chapter 7 the main managerial tasks that relate to patients and relatives, and are performed at the point of service delivery, were described. This chapter examines specific problems, associated with the management of patients, clients and relatives, as they arise in different spheres of medicine.

Paediatrics

Case 2

Emma, aged 6, was admitted to hospital for a middle ear infection. She came from a middle class environment, with intelligent, caring parents. They were very anxious as this was the first time Emma had come into contact with doctors (apart from the GP) and nurses; the first time she had encountered such things as injections; and the first time she had slept away from home.

(1) How could she, and her parents, have been prepared for her admission to hospital?
(2) Who might best undertake such preparation?

Emma has one sibling, a boy of 4 years called Michael. They have always been very close and Michael depends on Emma to help, teach and, to some extent, protect him. Now he feels lost and his parents, in their anxiety about Emma, do not seem to be aware of his pain and anxiety.

(3) How do you think Michael is feeling?
(4) What may be his feelings towards Emma?
(5) How would you recognise Michael's feelings? How might they reveal themselves?
(6) How could you help Emma? Michael? The parents?

Case 3

John is aged 12. He is an intelligent boy who has a brain tumour. This has been treated with chemotherapy and is now being treated with radiotherapy. He is not responding well to treatment and his prognosis is very poor. His parents are distraught and unable to comprehend what is happening. Their way of coping is to telephone frequently for information, but to avoid visiting, which they find too painful. John has on several occasions tried to talk to the nurses about dying and death, but has not yet been able to do so to his satisfaction, partly because of lack of time, partly because of lack of privacy and partly because of constant interruptions by other children. He has raised the subject with his parents but their reaction was 'Don't be silly! Of course you're not going to die!'

(1) How can you best help John?
(2) Who might you call on to help him?
(3) How could you encourage the parents to visit?
(4) How can you provide help and support for the parents so that they can come to terms with John's condition and feel able to talk to him about it?
(5) What do you know about children's and adolescents' reaction to dying and death?

Jane, aged 14, has been diagnosed as diabetic and will require insulin by injection for life. She has been discharged from hospital and you have understood that she can deal with her own injections. The GP is concerned that she is not doing this adequately, and, as she comes from a one-parent family, and her mother works, you have been asked to call on her and assess the situation. When you visit you find:

- that she fears injections and from time to time fails to give herself the evening injection
- that she has developed a school phobia as she feels more secure at home.

(1) How would you deal with Jane? Her mother? Jane's fear of injections? Jane's school phobia?
(2) Who might you involve in the problem of the school phobia?

Paediatric wards, and the treatment of sick children generally, have changed considerably within the last two decades. Parents are encouraged to stay with children, the importance of play as a therapeutic and cathartic activity has been recognised, and play assistants, working with teachers, are to be found in most childrens' wards. Nursing staff have, in many places, discarded uniforms in favour of brightly coloured aprons, although medical staff are less anxious to discard white coats! There are still, however, a number of areas in the field of paediatrics where communication and the management of patients, clients and relatives need to be examined.

1. Children in hospital

Figure 15 shows some of the relationships and communication patterns of the child in hospital.

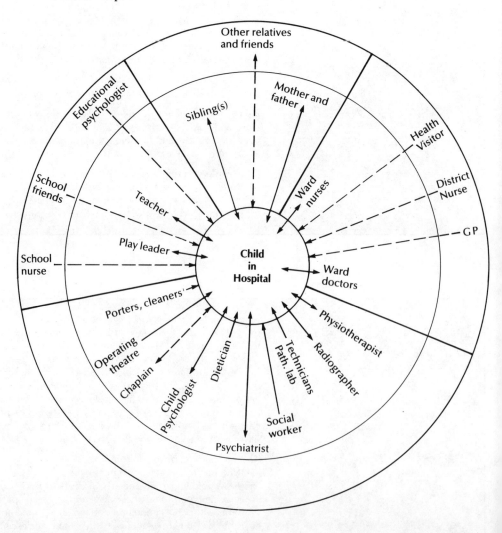

Figure 15   The child in hospital

1.1 How are children prepared for admission?

There are now several very helpful publications for parents that explain what happens when children are admitted. One of these, *Your Child in Hospital*, is published by the National Association for the Welfare of Children in Hospital, 7, Exton Street, London N7.

Community and GP nurses and school nurses are especially concerned with helping to prepare children, and many hospitals prepare their own booklets, which are helpful.

1.2 The reaction of the family

Siblings

Siblings and their reactions to the admission of a loved brother or sister are, in the general anxiety, all too often forgotten, and their pain and anxiety ignored. Moreover, mother and father may be so concerned with the sick child that they become neglectful of the other(s). This can lead to anger against the parents or the sick child, and, if later, the sick child dies, the most terrible feelings of guilt. School nurses will probably meet with children who are suffering in this way and will be able to help. The illness of a child is very much a family affair. Hospital and community nurses should be aware of all the reactions that may occur and of the behaviour which may have, as its underlying cause, a deep anxiety or fear for the sick brother or sister. Feelings of 'Will I be next? Was it something I did? Will he/she die?' may result in atypical behaviour at school which the school nurse, if she is aware that a member of the family is sick, may be able to interpret and help resolve. This can only happen if there is close liaison between the various nursing staff concerned with the child, and if discussions take place to ensure that parents, the sick child and siblings are supported.

Many parents are afraid to allow siblings to be in the ward for too long in case they pick up infections, and indeed there is little point in doubling the number of children by having the whole family there all day long. Help should be offered to balance the psychological needs of the siblings with their health needs, and with the ability of the ward staff to cope with their presence. It may be that all the brother or sister wants is to see his or her sibling from time to time to make sure that he or she is getting better.

Parents

Not all parents are 'good' parents. Even those who make the right noises may not be the most caring.

Many things can be discovered about children while they are in hospital, and in the communications that take place between children and medical staff. These are all part of the management of patients and clients, and of the education of parents, which nurses are especially concerned with.

Not all parents have a sufficient level of intelligence to be able to understand easily the needs of sick children. Some do not care enough to do so, and many are young and have much to learn about children, sick or well. Sadly the learning may take place after their children have suffered considerably. Here is a golden opportunity to educate parents for the future. Paediatric nurses have the expertise to do this, and many parents would value the help which they can be given.

The majority of parents are, however, caring and loving, even if some of them are not able to show such emotions easily, and they need considerable help to come to terms with the sickness of their child. In most hospitals, one or other of the parents is encouraged to stay overnight, and to be there when the child goes to the theatre, or needs comforting through a painful treatment.

Children will bring in with them their 'comfort blankets' and their favourite toys, and will feel that the nurse is a friend and an ally.

General medicine and surgery

MacLeod-Clark[1] claims that patients' communication needs fall into seven categories:

● social interaction

- information
- advice
- re-assurance
- discussion of diagnosis, treatment and prognosis
- discussion of feelings
- counselling.

In this section of the book we will look at each of these categories of communication needs as they apply to different areas of medical care in community and hospital settings. The study examines a variety of cases that have been observed or reported to the author.

1. Social interaction

Case 5

Nurse: Do you like being in a six-bedded ward?
Patient 1: Yes, it's nice to have other people to talk to.
Patient 2: It's OK, but it gets a bit noisy at night, what with her over there talking in her sleep, and him snoring!

(1) In a ward with six-bedded bays and single rooms:
  (a) Who decides where each patient is put?
  (b) On what criteria is such a decision made?
  (c) Do you think these criteria are justified?
  (d) Are the patients ever consulted, or is this not possible?
(2) How important do you think social interaction is in hospital?
(3) What benefits do patients gain from being in a multi-bedded ward? A single room?
(4) How do patients react to mixed sex wards? Have they been asked? What provision can be made for the person who dislikes mixed sex wards?

2. Information

Case 6

'Do you know what is wrong with you?'
'Oh, yes! I've got a wheezy chest.'
'Do you know what causes that?'
'It's something to do with my heart, I think.'
'Would you like to know more?'
'Yes, I would really. They don't tell you everything. Mind you, it's probably better you don't know!'

(1) What do you think of this conversation?
(2) Do you ever ask patients 'Is there anything else you want to know?'
(3) How can you decide whether a patient should be told about his or her condition?
(4) Do patients ever truly not wish to know about their condition?

Case 7

'It's a nice friendly hospital. I can ask the doctors anything, but I'm not cheeky, mind! They expect you to do as you are told don't they? The little nurses are lovely, but they work so hard. I try not to worry them with too many questions.'
What does this tell you about:

- The medical and nursing staff?
- The atmosphere of the hospital?
- The patient's expectations and attitudes?

3. Advice

Case 8

An elderly lady with a heart condition is about to be discharged from the ward. The doctor says to her 'Now Mrs Jones, you can go home tomorrow. You will have to be very careful not to overdo it, and not to climb any stairs. You will fix that up Sister, won't you?' When the doctor has left, the old lady is bewildered and frightened. She says to the patient in the next bed 'It's all very well for him, but I live on my own and I've got to look after myself and I can't help going up stairs, I sleep there!'

(1) How will the Sister re-assure the old lady about the future?
(2) What can the Sister do to ensure that the doctor's instructions can be carried out?
(3) List the people the Sister will have to contact to make the arrangements?
(4) Do you think it is reasonable to expect the old lady to go home next day? What can the Sister do about that?

4. Re-assurance

Case 9

A patient is given a tablet that he has not seen before. He says, 'Are you sure that this is my tablet, nurse? I've never seen it before.'
  'It's quite right Mr Smith.'
  'What's it for?'
  'It'll make you feel better.'
  'Does that mean that I'm getting worse?'
  'No, of course it doesn't Mr Smith, it's just that the doctor thought you needed something stronger.'
  'It **must** mean that I'm getting worse, then! Why else would the doctor make the dose stronger?'
  'Why don't you ask him when he comes round?'
  'He'll only tell me the same as you!'
  The nurse laughs, preferring to accept this comment as an attempt at jocularity on the part of the patient.

(1) Discuss this exchange.
    (a) How do you think the patient felt?
    (b) How might the nurse have answered the patient?
(2) Role play the situation. How did you feel, as the patient, when you got these responses? Try it again, using the responses you suggested at (1).

Case 10

Two nurses are making a patient's bed.
  Patient: I had a friend who had a pain in her belly just like mine, but she had cancer, not an ulcer like me. She died.
  Nurse: What a shame! I expect you missed her, didn't you?
  Patient: Yes, it's funny we should both end up with stomach trouble, isn't it?
  Nurse: Yes.

What was the patient really saying?
Do you think she got the re-assurance she was seeking?

Case 11

A nurse has just been packing a patient's things ready for her move to another ward. The patient says, 'Why am I being moved?'
  'It's a ward specially for gastric patients.'
  'Oh!'
  The nurse leaves and the patient says to her neighbour, 'What do you think about that? Do you think there's something they aren't telling me?'
  'Why don't you ask Sister?'
  'I don't like to. She might think I'm complaining.'

Many questions go unasked because the patient does not wish to be seen as complaining, holding up the work of the ward or showing a lack of trust in the staff. Schwartz[2], in 1958, working in out-patient's clinics, claimed that the 'unpopular' patients were those who:

● found it difficult to conform to clinic routine
● demanded attention in apparently excessive amounts
● required immediate gratification of requests
● responded immaturely to any pressures
● possessed, to a remarkable degree, the ability to 'needle' the professionally prepared people.

Patients **can** be very demanding, very irritating and apparently lacking in maturity, and it is the quiet, patient and uncomplaining patient who is most popular with the staff, and who has most staff time spent on her. **It is, however, the frightened, difficult patient who needs most care and attention, but who frequently has least staff attention.**

5. Discussion of diagnosis, treatment and prognosis

Case 12	The Consultant has just told the patient that she is to have a 'little operation'. She asks, 'What exactly are you going to do?'
	The Consultant looks somewhat surprised and his attendant 'flock' smile, somewhat patronisingly. He replies, 'You don't need to worry about that. Just you leave it to us. We'll look after you.' He pats her gently on the arm.
	The patient says, 'I'm sure you will, but just the same I **would** like to know what you are going to do.'
	The Consultant, with a barely concealed sigh, sits on her bed and says, 'We are going to do a cholecystectomy because your bile duct is obstructed by an irremovable object.'
	The patient replies, 'What is a **chole** ... chol ... whatever it was you said?'
	The Consultant, forced to explain more simply, took out a pad and pencil and drew a quite reasonable diagram, and, getting interested himself, said, 'We join your gall bladder, this thing here, to your small intestine, here. This lets the bile pass from the liver directly into the intestine. We have to do that because this tube, the common bile duct as it is called, is blocked, probably by gall stones.'
	The patient says, 'Thank you that is quite clear now. I am very grateful to you for explaining it so clearly.'

This patient was intelligent enough to insist, quietly and politely, on an answer. This does not mean that the only patients deserving an explanation are those who will insist on one. In fact it is the diffident or frightened or less intelligent ones who are probably most in need of such care and help. **Whose body is it anyway?**

Case 13	A physiotherapist is trying to get a reluctant patient, who has had abdominal surgery, to cough.
	Physio: Now come on Mrs Jones, take a deep breath and cough.
	The patient is still smarting from the thumping she has just received! 'It's very painful, nurse.'
	Physio: I'm **not** a nurse. I'm a physiotherapist. Now come on. I know it hurts a bit but it's for your own good. Put your hands over your wound and give a big cough.
	The patient, close to tears, says, 'Well I don't know who you are, you all look the same to me! I'll try.' She gives a feeble cough which does nothing to help her rattling chest.
	(1) How would **you** encourage this patient to cough?
	(2) Is 'bullying', in the patient's own interest, ever realistic and/or necessary?
	(3) Why did the patient think the physiotherapist was a nurse? How could this have been avoided?

Exercise 22

(1) Re-read the section on listening skills.
(2) What is the importance of 'the music behind the words' and the unspoken message inherent in the communication and hinted at in the non-verbal communication or the use of words, phrases or expressions?
(3) Consider the expression 'Familiarity breeds contempt'. One of the failings of those working in specialist areas such as medicine is that, because **they** understand jargon, medical and anatomical terms, and the epidemiology of illness, they sometimes forget that the patients may not be familiar with them.
(4) Over the next few weeks listen to patients describing, either to each other or to other patients, what they think is wrong with them.
(5) Note the terms they use – for example, 'I've got an ulcer in my back passage.'
(6) Note how accurate their knowledge of anatomy is. You can ask patients to point out where they think their heart, stomach, liver or spleen are.
(7) When a doctor has given some information to a patient, ask her what she has understood the doctor to have said. How accurate is her understanding?

6. Discussion of feelings and the use of counselling skills

Case 14

It was a quiet time in the four-bedded bay. The patients were talking quietly to each other or listening to their radios. Suddenly a young new housewoman appeared, obviously under some strain. With an anxious expression she looked around the bay, muttered something under her breath, and moved quickly from bed to bed, picking up and looking at each chart, and writing on two of them. She then looked around again, went to one woman and said, 'Can I just look at your eyes?' She pulled down the lower eyelid and muttered something which sounded like 'Humph!'

The patient said, 'Is everything OK, doctor?'

'Yes,' she responded, smiling absently as she wrote on the woman's chart. With a final look around and another muttered word, she left. The patients looked at each other:

'Who was that?'

'New doctor.'

'What do you think she wanted?'

'I wonder why she looked at my eyes?'

'I wonder what she wrote on my chart?'

The previously peaceful ward had reached a high level of anxiety.

Discuss.

Ignoring patients can sometimes be worse than any other form of non-verbal communication. It says 'I'm too busy to bother with you' or 'You're not someone I have time for.'

Case 15

This is an exchange between a tough-looking man and the nurse.

Nurse: I'll come and give you an injection later.

Patient: Much later!

Nurse: Yes, about 11 o'clock.

Note that the patient's response was an exclamation, **not** a question.

(1) What do you think he was trying to say?
(2) Can you judge a patient's ability to cope with even a small amount of pain by his appearance?

Case 16

A senior nurse is discovered giving medicines to the patients. She has her back to them and is concentrating on being very accurate, teaching the learner who is with her how to carry out this important procedure. At the same time she is using the time to do a round of the patients and ask how they are. She comes to one man, who

looks most uncomfortable, and, looking at him over her shoulder, she says, 'All right Mr Smith?'
Mr Smith: Not really nurse, I've . . .
Nurse: Good!
This case demonstrates some important points:

● It is very difficult to remember everything.
● It is vital to be accurate about giving medicines, and nothing should interfere with this accuracy.
● It is also very damaging to **ask** a patient how he or she is and then fail to listen to the response. Teaching by demonstrating is the best way to make sure that learners understand the importance of what you are doing. **You** are a role model for learners. When they see you paying little attention to a patient, they might be tempted to react in the same way at some future time. How can you reconcile these demands on your attention?

Exercise 23

A woman has been admitted for treatment of hepatitis. While admitting her and discussing the nursing history, it becomes obvious that the patient is concerned, not especially about her condition, but about her home and those she has left behind. At this time the nurse finds herself using counselling skills to discover what is worrying the patient and to assess the help the patient will require. The problems are:

● She has two teenage children, a boy of 15 and a girl of 13.
● The boy has been rather wild in the past and, without his mother's presence, may take up with the companions who have led him into scrapes in the past. He drinks, sometimes to excess, gambles on fruit machines and, at one time, sniffed glue. Lately he has settled down at school and is much more controllable. His drinking is less and he has, for the time being, stopped gambling.
● The father drinks quite heavily and, when the mother is not present, could become out of control.
● The daughter is the mainstay of her mother, but she may be in some danger from the father if left at home. These worries are not immediately given to the nurse, but she can see clearly the anxiety of the patient.

At present she thinks that the patient is anxious about her condition.
Role play in threes: A, B and C. A becomes the nurse, B becomes the patient and C becomes the observer. A does not know what is concerning the patient. Her script only tells her the diagnosis of the patient, and that she is aware that there is something worrying her. B has a script that tells her of the problems the patient has. C does not know what is concerning the patient. Her job is to:

(1) Identify which counselling skills A exhibits.
(2) Give A feedback at the end of the role play which will comment on how effectively she dealt with the patient. She **must** not speak during the role play.
(3) See whether the real anxieties are discovered by A.

Elderly care

Most people work throughout life, arrive at some level of status in which they can take pride and produce some work which is valued by someone. Regardless of how menial or humble the work, we can take some pride in doing it to the best of our ability, of feeling needed by someone and, if we are fortunate enough, of leaving something that we have accomplished and is valued after we have ceased to work.

It is unfortunate that, during our working lives, few managers ever take the time to praise our efforts, although they rarely hesitate to correct our mistakes! This lack of appreciation can be reinforced by the way we are treated following retirement.

Most elderly people have a young person inside them trying to get out! They may not feel much different mentally at 70 than they did at 40, except that they may have learned more patience and how to relate to people more effectively! They do not, therefore, appreciate being treated as though they need a nanny, nor do they, as they become progressively more helpless, appreciate having their disabilities stressed by being constantly asked 'Can you manage?' or 'Let **me** do that!' These 'kindnesses' simply make them more aware of their increasing helplessness and of the fact that they are of apparently little use to anyone. 'If I want help, I'll ask!' one old lady was heard to say. The response by her nurse was 'Miserable old thing!'

Nurses are constantly being reminded that they should respect the dignity of the older patient. Most of them are very conscious of this need, but it is all too easy, when an old person falls about, mumbles, dribbles her food, is incontinent and generally behaves like an untrained baby, to remember that she **still** has the right to be treated with respect, and the little dignity that her disabilities will allow, preserved. Even the senile old lady, seemingly divorced from reality, has moments of conscious understanding and can say sadly 'Oh, nurse I'm so sorry. I've made my bed wet again.' How many of the tears that the old shed are shed because of the realisation of what they have become and what they have lost?

To have lost respect and dignity is to have lost the last element in the human condition that divides the thinking, planning part of the being from the animal part, the basis of our being and its baser component.

Case 17	A nurse, speaking to old lady, says 'Come on now gran, stand up!'
	'I'm not your gran! Anyway I haven't got any children. Why do you call me gran?'
	'What shall we call you then? I know, we'll call you Mary! That's your name isn't it?'
	'My name is Miss Roberts, and don't you forget it. You cheeky young madam.'
	Miss Roberts mumbled for a long time, becoming more and more confused, and eventually shouting out 'She's cheeky that one, don't you talk to her. Keep away from me!' and so on.
	Eventually she became very disturbed and had to be given a sedative.

Another aspect of getting old is that of anticipating, sometimes fearing and coming to terms with death. Old age has been described as the waiting room to death, but most people live a lively, interesting and productive retirement. This does, of course, depend on physical and mental fitness, adequate diet, adequate money to be able to have the means to give some quality to life and social contacts that will enable the old person to continue to take an interest in the world.

When children no longer care and many friends have died or gone to live elsewhere, there seems nothing in life worth waiting for; death seems a friend to be welcomed, rather than an enemy to be avoided. Unfortunately, for those people, death may refuse to offer release. The bitterness and unhappiness may be seen as a poor reward for a lifetime of hard and devoted work for children, employers and the community. Nurses often bear the burden of such bitterness. They are told 'You'll understand one day!', and no doubt this may be true, but meanwhile their management of the patient or client will involve their most sensitive efforts in encouraging participation in active mental and physical activities, in ensuring that good diet is taken, and in trying to restore and maintain the shattered self-esteem.

Intensive care units, coronary care units, renal units, oncology wards and other high-stress areas

Nursing, *per se*, is a very stressful occupation, and the nurse who is dealing with his or her own painful memories, and who meets with similar cases at work, will be under increased and possibly unendurable stress. A nurse whose grandmother had recently died, on return from the funeral, was put almost immediately on to a geriatric ward and had to watch the death of other old women. One in particular reminded her of her grandmother and she was reprimanded for sitting for long periods holding the dying old lady's hand and neglecting the work of the ward. Her manager said that she was unaware that the girl's grandmother had died, but then added 'Even so I think that it is good that she should be on this ward. It will give her a chance to come to terms with it, and it will make her more sympathetic with the relatives.' Unfortunately the grieving that the girl should have been doing was buried under the need to be 'professional' and to conceal her feelings.

With a shortage of nursing staff it is not possible to enquire too closely into every possible sensitivity a nurse may have, but the obvious errors, such as the one quoted, **should** be avoided. It should also be remembered that even after a year, which is usually given as the minimum time the bereaved person takes to come to some form of resolution, 'unfinished business' can still strike unexpectedly, and when this happens the manager's responsibility is to help the nurse understand what has happened and, if necessary, refer the nurse for some further counselling help.

Having said that nurses are vulnerable to stress in every kind of ward and community situation, it is obvious that there are undoubtedly areas where stress is heightened by the life-threatening conditions of the patients, of its painful or unpleasant manifestations, or of the length of time involved when one patient is on the ward for many weeks or even months. One of the first management tasks of the nurse manager working in these areas is to support and maintain those who work with him or her.

The September 1988 issue of *The Nursing Times* (pages 26–30) gave some interesting information about counselling services available to nurses. Even more interesting was an article (pages 30–32 of the same journal) that described the way in which the staff of the ICU at Addenbrook's Hospital had responded to the stress of working in that environment, how they consciously supported each other when they saw evidence of stress and, more importantly, how this was done on a continuing multi-disciplinary basis, which helped dissipate stress and spot it before it became an insurmountable problem. It is a matter of watching out for each other, and of understanding, without being told, why a nurse becomes 'snappy' or fails to give the usual calm and helpful answers you have come to expect, and, when you see such a manifestation of stress, of giving special attention and help.

When they have been carefully introduced to ICU nursing, and are well supervised, most nurses enjoy the work and gain considerably from it. In such a unit the nurse will have total care of one patient. At first the nurse may be somewhat bemused and anxious about the amount of equipment and the great responsibility of caring for a patient whose life may be totally dependent on him or her, but he or she will find that here much of the learning gained elsewhere is co-ordinated.

Concentrating on accurate observations and watching for subtle changes in a patient's condition is very tiring and stressful. Long nights without the relief of being able to talk to the patients give the nurse a responsibility that is heavy to bear. Support from peers and the nurse manager is the only way in which these stresses can be dealt with.

Case 18

A woman of 50 was admitted unconscious to an ICU having suffered a severe cerebrovascular accident. She was being ventilated and appeared to be in a very deep coma. It was not thought that she would recover, and the medical staff were beginning to contemplate stopping treatment. The nurse who looked after her noticed that, when a discussion of this kind had taken place at the foot of her bed, the patient became very restless. The nurse felt that the patient was aware of what was being said and she discussed this with the two housemen who had had the discussion. Some weeks later the patient recovered from her coma. She was ultimately, with difficulty, able to communicate and told the nurse that she had had many 'dreams', one of which was that someone was planning to kill her. It cannot be said with certainty that this was related to the discussion between the housemen, but the patient also remembered a number of things that she had heard while in her coma, and was able to quote them.

Case 19

A man of 60 was admitted to the ICU having suffered a stroke, which had rendered him aphonic, although he could make some noises. He often became very irritable and shouted at the nurses. When fed, he had a habit of spitting out the food put in his mouth. It was observed that the nurses gave him significantly less time than was given to other patients. When he was communicated with, many of the nurses spoke to him loudly, as though he was deaf, or used simple 'baby' talk. On one occasion a nurse was feeding him and insisted on putting food in his mouth, even though he had twice turned his head away. On the third occasion he spat the food all over her. She gave his hand a playful slap and said 'Oh you are a naughty boy Mr Smith!'

(1) What do you think causes the irritability and spitting?
(2) How should this patient be handled?

Role play in pairs: A and B. A is blindfolded and B leads A around:

- holding A by the arm but not speaking
- taking A around the room and describing what the room is like, letting A touch the walls or other surfaces, to get some idea of the different textures, and letting A smell any flowers, etc.

Get a wheel chair for a day and wheel each other around noticing how you are treated, and what problems there are for those in wheel chairs.

(1) How does sensory deprivation feel?
(2) What emotions does it arouse?
(3) What do you think people with different kinds of sensory deprivation seek from their nurses?

Patients in ICUs and CCUs must feel very imprisoned by being tied down by lines, leads and catheters, and hemmed in by equipment. They have lost their autonomy and need to regain it. This can be done by explaining what is being done to them, telling them how they can help and letting them do as much for themselves as they possibly can.

Those who are deprived of sight need to be told who is approaching them. All patients in shuttered areas, where lights burn day and night, need to be kept orientated as to the time, date, day and what is happening around them.

Apparently unconscious patients may be able to hear. They should be talked **to** and never talked **about** within hearing distance.

Relatives may feel very concerned that, when their loved one most needs them, they have to leave the care to 'strangers'. Their frustration can be shown by being demanding, seeking constant re-assurance or even by being hostile. Many relatives also feel guilty that they may not have done enough for their loved one while in their care, and this may also make them react to nursing staff in a hostile or difficult manner.

Confusion and hallucinations can be very distressing to a sick person. There may be little that can be done, but the nurse should be there to offer comfort and support. Patients need the human touch. Holding or stroking a patient's hand, especially if that person is restless, and even unconscious, will give much comfort.

Nurse managers should be able to:

- **recognise** those patients who need company and support
- **develop** observational skills and learn to empathise
- **assess** the need that patients have for information.

| **Case 20** | Relatives were observed removing the oxygen face mask from a patient, presumably because they could not hear what he was trying to tell them. The nurse rushed over to the patient and said rather angrily, 'You mustn't touch the equipment.'
One of the relatives said, 'He doesn't like that thing on his face nurse.'
'Well, like it or not it's for his own good!' replied the nurse.
How might the relatives have been better dealt with? |

Oncology patients also have some very special needs.

| **Case 21** | A 40-year old woman was admitted to an oncology unit with a breast cancer. At operation it was found that she had extensive spread of the tumour, and it was decided that she should have chemotherapy, possibly followed by radiotherapy. She had two children, aged 14 and 9, and her husband was the manager of the local electricity showroom. She was constantly asking the nurses about her condition, although the doctor had told her about it. She also talked to the other patients who |

got rather annoyed that she was always asking about dying and death. The nurses who she met with most frequently were the junior nurses on the ward. Most of the other nurses stayed as far out of her way as they could. On one occasion, when she was particularly distressed, one of the junior nurses was heard to say, 'There, there, it'll be all right you know. The doctors are very good here.'

She replied, 'But nobody will tell me whether I am going to get better or not, and I can't decide how to talk to Bill (her husband) about the children!'

The nurse said, 'Well, I don't expect they know much more than you do! Doctors and nurses don't have **all** the answers you know!'

The behaviour of the patient became more and more disruptive to the rest of the ward's patients and so she was moved into a single room, which she was discouraged from leaving, on the grounds that other patients needed rest and should not be disturbed. She was also given a television set 'to keep her occupied!' Her husband said that her behaviour was not typical as his wife had always been a quiet, rather diffident lady.

Atypical behaviour may give a clue to the fact that the patient is anxious and wishes to find out more about his or her condition. Nurses should not be reluctant to find out what is worrying a patient, and should ask such questions as:

- Are you worried about anything at home or at work?
- Are you worried about your children (or wife, or husband, or cat, or anything else)?
- When you have problems, how do you usually sort them out?
- Why can't you do that now?
- What **specific** information could I give you which would help you?
- Do you have a special friend who you could talk to?
- Would you like to have the opportunity to speak in private with the doctor (or the priest, or the social worker)?

Oncology patients are usually concerned about becoming permanent invalids, being disfigured (particularly young women who have had a mastectomy) and, of course, dying. Nurses are often afraid to tell patients their diagnosis and prognosis as they feel that this is the province of the doctor. Nurse managers have a responsibility to ensure that policies are decided with the consultants concerned, which will give guidelines to nurses about what is expected of them in giving information to patients and relatives. They should also ensure that the kind of questions that arise are well known, and that they know the answers.

Case 22

Mr Smith was dying at home with terminal carcinoma. He was visited by a neighbour who asked him how he was.

'Well, I'm not too bad in myself, but I'm not very happy about Edie (his wife).'

'Why?'

'Well, I know I'm dying, but I can't talk to her about it, and there are so many things I want to tell her. Every time I try she puts her hands over her ears and says "Don't talk like that. You're **not** going to die, I won't listen to you." Do you think you could talk to her?'

'Why don't you tell the MacMillan nurse? She knows Edie better than I do and would help.'

'I don't like her very much. She doesn't listen when I try to tell her. She's very nice I'm sure, but I've never really liked her.' [NB However 'nice' not everyone can relate to everyone else. Nurses should recognise any antipathy and suggest a replacement.]

'What about the Health Visitor?'

'Yes she was nice, but she doesn't come now that the MacMillan nurse comes, and the District Nurse is always in such a rush.'

The neighbour spoke to the daughter, but she said that she had tried to get her mother to talk to her father without success. Mr Smith died without being able to talk to his wife, and she was devastated by his death which she had been denying, not only to him but to herself.

What help could have been given to help Mrs Smith come to terms with her husband's impending death?

AIDS units

AIDS patients face all the problems of oncology patients, but they also have others which nurse managers should make sure nurses are aware of:

- They face the loss of job, friends, wife, husband or lover.
- They face the loss of their usual expression of sexuality.
- They know that, at present, there is no cure for AIDS.
- Their condition is very much feared, and the fear of infection by those who look after them, although not a likely thing to occur, must be at the forefront of the carers' minds. The important thing is not to place the AIDS patient in the position of feeling like a leper. If nurses understand the nature of the disease, they will be able to tell when and what extra care is needed, and so prevent the pain that the young man must have felt.
- They may have been subjected to punitive or cruel taunting, or to attitudes that have made their lives miserable.
- They may have to face particularly unpleasant symptoms.
- They will have to tell their lovers or spouses, who may not be able to cope with the knowledge.
- Even if they have only been tested for HIV, and have been found negative, they will not be granted a mortgage or be allowed to insure their lives. (Note that nurses must be educated in the epidemiology, care and treatment of patients and clients with a positive HIV.)

Psychiatric and mental handicap units

This is the area in which the need for good communication should be best understood as the nurses in these units are trained in, and use, counselling and psychotherapy. Where such nurses proceed to general training they often demonstrate a much clearer view of the psychological needs of patients and can be consulted by other nurses to offer advice about those patients who need special help and understanding.

Burr and Budge[3] suggested five objectives when talking to psychiatric patients:

- To create a relationship of trust and confidence.
- To help patients put their problems into words.
- To draw patients back from their world of fantasy.
- To re-assure patients and relieve tension.
- To help patients talk to other people and make normal conversation.

To attain these objectives the counselling skills of empathy, reflecting, recall and feedback, using questions, summarising, accurate listening (attending) and closure are used. Most of these have already been described in earlier chapters, and it would be helpful to re-read those sections.

Terminal care

The care of the dying patient and the relatives is of such importance that it will only be possible here to summarise some of the most important points. There are many very helpful books that can be read for further information, but the nurse should remember that this is a condition that will overtake all of us at some time, and that his or her responsibility is not only to prevent and cure illness, but also to help those coming to the end of life, to leave it as easily and comfortably as possible. In fact, this is one of the greatest privileges that nursing offers.

Much has already been said about the importance of this care, the final, loving act that a nurse can provide for a patient. It has been said that doctors and nurses are 'curers', and that they may feel that the death of a patient is a personal failure. Such attitudes may persist in some places, but so much importance has been placed on this aspect of patient care in recent years that it must now be only rarely encountered. What nurse managers must now be aware of is how to help their staff to put into practice what they are taught. One of the difficulties of doing this is that death and dying are such a part of all our lives that our instinct is to avoid, as far as possible, thinking or talking about them.

Nurses often dread the necessity of telling patients and relatives the 'bad' news. They will use many subterfuges to avoid doing so, often being themselves unaware that this is what they are doing. They need help to come to terms with these feelings. The training offered to nurses at present is very inadequate. It ranges from a minimal 'care of the dying' component in the basic training to the English National Board (ENB) 913 'Care of the dying and the family' courses mounted at specially selected hospitals, and available to only a few nurses. It seems obvious that every nurse should be well tutored in the art of caring in this area of nursing.

One way that has been used to bridge the gap in the provision of training was instituted in 1982 at Basingstoke, where the National Society for Cancer Relief financed the appointment of two MacMillan nurses for three years. These nurses were not given the usual case load but were attached to the district to respond to any member of staff, wherever he or she worked, who had a problem with a dying patient. They worked with the staff, teaching and demonstrating good practice, and crossing the boundaries of hospital and community to ensure continuity of care, and the continuing care of relatives. Along with other tutors they provided an educational function for learners and for in-service trainers. Requests for help came from GPs, community and hospital nurses, and ancillary workers at all levels, to provide:

● practical nursing advice and equipment
● advice on pain and symptom control
● assistance in relieving distress in patients, relatives and **staff caring for the terminally ill** (a most important aspect of their work).

The **replacement** of hospice or MacMillan nurses was **not** an objective of this initiative; its aim was to ensure that all those caring for the terminally ill would be able, with support, to care for them in a sensitive and confident manner, and to offer a co-ordinated approach. This pattern is now followed at many hospitals.

It is suggested that one of the main needs of the dying person is to talk about the condition of dying, and about the situation that will arise in the family as a result of one of its members being removed. It will depend, of course, on whether the dying is sudden or protracted. In the latter case the main preoccupations will be with the possibility of pain, loss of independence, separation from loved ones and leaving some project upon which the person was engaged, unfinished.

Death is sometimes seen, either by the patient or by a relative, as a punishment for past wickedness. These feelings should be explored and discussed. In other words, as in every other area of the human state, the state of dying and death is affected profoundly by good satisfying communication.

Community care

Nurses in the community usually enter into more enduring relationships than those to be found in hospital wards, where the constant turnover of patients and staff precludes such relationships. The client is also in a different relationship with the nurse, being on his or her own ground, and with the nurse as guest in the client's house. Also, relatives, who have been looking after a loved person for a long time, may resent the intrusion of the nurse. The nurse manager will take these factors into account when training new nurses who are to work in this very different field, and who may have been trained in a hospital ward where the nurse makes the 'rules'. In fact, the care of clients in their homes should be a shared responsibility between the District Nurse and the relatives.

The client will frequently employ a variety of tactics to avoid doing what the nurse asks. The nurse must learn to use tactics too! Generally speaking it is wisest to persuade by some tactical means rather than to insist on the grounds that it will 'do you good!'

It is very important to ensure that relatives are able to cope. Many of them find it a great burden to shoulder and become exhausted. Where a wife, for example, is obviously coming to the end of her tether, the nurse must find some way of persuading husband and wife that a short period in hospital would help her to recover, and continue the care with renewed vigour.

Community psychiatric nurses (CPNs) and community mental handicap nurses have special difficulties in monitoring the well being of those in their care and, to some extent, acting as 'protectors' of the community as a whole by recognising the need for further treatment if it arises. In addition they support, in the community, those who have been discharged from hospital and from units where they have previously been cared for. In the case of the mentally handicapped this will require a considerable expenditure of time and sensitive care, to enable the client to function on competitive terms with other members of the community, to maintain physical and mental well being, and, wherever possible, to continue in employment.

CPNs are a part of the psychiatric treatment team, which includes the hospital psychiatric nurse, the disablement resettlement officer, the psychoanalyst, the psychologist, the occupational therapist, the psychiatric social worker and the psychiatrist. Together with the patient and the patient's family they provide a comprehensive psychiatric service, liaising with:

● the hospital psychiatric unit
● the health centre
● specialist units
● sheltered workshops, day centres, clubs, hostels and half-way houses
● out-patient clinics
● day hospitals
● special hospital regional secure units.

They provide crisis intervention and, through the specialist units, offer help with alcoholics, drug addicts, children and adolescents with psychiatric problems. They are a very special and important part of the preventive, supportive and curative care of people in the community.

Black and ethnic minority patients or clients

No book on communications would be complete without consideration of one of the least well-managed areas of patient care. There is no doubt that prejudice and racism exist in most human beings. This is, at its least, pernicious, and leads to feelings of being undervalued and unwanted by these minority groups. At its worst, it leads to terrible suffering among the communities.

Within health care it is vital that workers of all disciplines and professions understand what prejudice and racism are, are enabled to come to terms with their own racist feelings, and are shown how these feelings can be translated into actions that can prove painful for the group or individual concerned and can affect the provision of care by offering care that would be unacceptable by others.

It is the job of the nurse manager to provide training and to help staff come to terms with feelings and attitudes that may be deeply ingrained. It is also the nurse manager's responsibility to ensure that patients and clients do not, in any way, suffer from such attitudes.

The perceptions that so many of us hold about our ethnic minority and black neighbours are stereotypes that are fed to us as children. They are mostly negative in character, and usually incorrect. They have to do with such stereotypes as:

- they all have large numbers of children
- they are dirty
- they always get the best houses and know how to get everything out of the social services
- they make more of a fuss about pain than white people
- most muggers and crooks are Afro-Caribbean in origin.

The truth is that most of the ethnic minority groups living in this country:

- tend to receive less consideration from the social services than their white cousins
- are less well housed
- are considered last when it comes to getting jobs
- have poorer health
- have a poorer diet
- are often victimised by their neighbours and other members of the community.

The truth, proved by research, is available. It is rarely believed by the ignorant and prejudiced, but nurses have taken very seriously the need to look at this area of their work.

Through the Asian Mother and Baby Campaign, much has been done to help correct dietary deficiencies, to draw attention to the need for screening for diseases specific to certain ethnic groups and the need to help Asian women who spoke no English to understand about health care and its provision in this country. The promotion of the latter initiative was considerably helped by the Linkworker scheme. Linkworkers are bi-lingual workers who, in addition to acting as interpreters, also have a responsibility, working with nurses, to help the Asian community understand and benefit from the provisions of the NHS. The schemes have been very successful and are being adopted by most of the districts with large ethnic minority or black groups.

What nurses need, in addition to an understanding of racism and its evils, is more factual information about diets, customs, religious beliefs and practices, and the culture of this group of citizens. In some districts this information has been provided by producing booklets for a wide range of ethnic groups.

Case 25	A nurse, speaking to black lady, said 'Where do you come from?' 'Brixton!' 'No, I don't mean that. Where do you really come from?' 'Well, I was born in Brixton, and my mother was born in Brixton, so I come from Brixton.' 'I expect you would like to visit your own country again one day wouldn't you?' 'This is my country!'

Case 26	A nurse speaking to Muslim lady who had given her name as Amina Begum said 'Good morning Mrs Begum.' The woman did not respond, as Begum is merely a female title meaning Ms! The nurse said, 'Mrs Begum? That is your name isn't it?' There was still no response, so the nurse looked pityingly at the patient, shrugged and muttered to her companion, 'I suppose she doesn't understand English. I do wish they'd learn. After all, when in Rome! We'd better call the baby, Baby Begum!'

Asian naming systems are different from other naming systems. Once understood they are not difficult, but most people cannot be bothered to find out and use them correctly. Many Asians have, in despair, given up and adopted the

English naming system, often after they have been entered in hospital records with their correct Asian names. The result can be chaotic and dangerous for the patient who, for example, has been identified as resistant to antibiotics in one set of notes, but not in the second set started when she gave her 'English' name. Such lack of care can be lethal. It is also hurtful that people think so little of you that they cannot even be bothered to find out what your name is.

It should be noted that the cases quoted here are not meant to teach managers, who are clinical experts and who will therefore be aware of these examples of poor practice. They are included to provide teaching examples for nurse managers to use in the ward or community teaching of learners.

References

1. J. MacLeod-Clark, *Communication in Nursing* (London: HM + M, 1981).
2. D. R. Schwartz, 'Uncooperative patients?', *American Journal of Nursing* **75,** 1958.
3. J. Burr and U. V. Budge, *Nursing the Psychiatric Patient* (Bailliere Tindall, 1976).

Suggested further reading

Gordon W. Allport, *The Nature of Prejudice* (Addison-Wesley, 1984).

E. Ellis Cashmore, *The Logic of Racism* (Allen & Unwin, 1987).

Edward A. Charlesworth and Ronald G. Nathan, *Stress Management – A Comprehensive Guide to Wellness* (Souvenir Press, 1982).

Charles A. Corr and Donna M. Corr, eds., *Hospice Care – Principles and Practice* (Faber & Faber, 1983).

Suzanne Foster and Pamela Smith, *Brief Lives – Living with the Death of a Child* (Arlington Books and Thames Television, 1987).

Alix Henley, *Asians in Britain – Caring for Muslims and their Families, Caring for Hindus and their Families, Caring for Sikhs and their Families* (National Extension College, for DHSS and the King Edward's Fund for London, 1982; 1983).

Jack Hayward, *Information – A Prescription Against Pain* (RCN and National Council of Nurses of the UK, Research Project Series 2, Number 5, 1975).

Judy H. Katz, *White Awareness* (University of Oklahoma Press, 1984).

E. Kubler-Ross, *On Death and Dying* (Tavistock Publications, 1973).

Brian Lemin, *First Line Nursing Management* (Pitman Medical, 1978).

Margaret Manning, *The Hospice Alternative – Living with Dying* (Condor Books/ Souvenir Press, 1984).

Peggy Martin, *Care of the Mentally Ill*, The Essentials of Nursing Series (Macmillan, 1987).

Isabel E. P. Menzies, *Social Systems as a Defence Against Anxiety* (Tavistock Institute of Human Relations, 1981).

Colin Murray Parkes, *Studies of Grief in Adult Life* (Pelican Books, 1980).

Beverley Raphael, *The Anatomy of Bereavement,* Chapter 4 (Hutchinson, 1984).

B. Schoenberg, A. C. Carr, D. Peretz and D. D. S. Kutscher, eds., *Loss and Grief – Psychological Management in Medical Practice* (Columbia University Press, 1970).

E. Mark Stern, ed., *Psychotherapy and the Grieving Patient* (Harrington Park Press, 1985).

Felicity Stockwell, *The Unpopular Patient* (RCN and National Council of Nurses of the UK, Research Project Series 1, Number 2, 1972).

John Twitchin and Clare Demuth, *Multi-cultural Education* (BBC, 1981).

Jennifer Wilson-Barnett, *Stress in Hospital* (Churchill Livingstone, 1979).

Care of the dying, A guide for Health Authorities (NAHA, 1987).

Talking with Patients – A Teaching Approach (Observations of the Nuffield Provincial Hospitals Trust, 1980).

Health Visiting and School Nursing Reviewed (Health Visitors Association, 1987).

Neighbourhood Nursing – A Focus for Care, Report of the Community Nursing Review (HMSO, 1986).

Concluding remarks

In 1985 a report was sent to the NHS training authority which dealt with the use of the *Caring Communications* training package, originally prepared by Joanna Gray. This report looked at the form of the package, its use, and the possibility of its revision and re-issue.[1]

In the course of the extensive research carried out for this report, the reports of the Health Service Commissioner for England, Wales and Scotland, from 1976 to 1984, were read and analysed. It was difficult to obtain a complete set of these reports. This was thought regrettable, as the reports were most revealing as to the kind of treatment patients and clients may meet with in the course of their treatment, and should be of value in avoiding inappropriate or insensitive treatment.

Details of some 599 cases were given, of which 348 (58%) were found to be directly or indirectly caused by a failure of communication, or by inadequate communication. The most commonly expressed perceptions of nurses by complainants were: 'Nurses were seen as lacking concern, of being 'hard' and of providing inadequate care.' The Health Service Commissioner said of these complaints: **'In most cases these accusations were unjustified but were made because nurses failed to explain why certain procedures were followed or why, for example, patients were encouraged to get out and walk when they felt they could not do so.'** It is sad that a failure in communication can result in unjust and inaccurate perceptions of a generally devoted and caring profession.

This study alone provided overwhelming proof of the need for every discipline, at every level in the Health Service, to be alerted to the need for training in the skills of communication. This training should begin at the moment the individual enters training, and should continue throughout that person's professional life.

This book has looked at three areas of communication:

(1) Communication – the psychology and the skills of communication in society generally.
(2) Communication and communication skills as they affect first-line management, with special reference to the tasks of management.
(3) Skilled communication in the area of nurse management at the point of the delivery of care.

Many of these subjects can only be touched upon and, for this reason, a list of some of the most interesting and helpful books and reports have been given at the end of each chapter, which, it is hoped, will encourage nurse managers to pursue the art of better management through better communications.

It is recognised that it is comparatively easy to **tell** someone how to do things better when removed from the rough and tumble of working life. For this reason, a number of exercises and suggestions have been offered which may help nurses to recognise how and where they can improve their skills, and thus enhance their ability and career progression. Nurses are expected to become more skilful every day in a variety of areas, clinical and otherwise. Whatever can be done, therefore, to help an often hard-pressed profession, can only be of value.

The communication skills that can be of most help are:

- counselling support for nurses with stress and anxiety problems
- the realisation that ward sisters, or senior managers, are role models for learners, and therefore must take great care to ensure that their behaviour is congruent with the image the public expects of a nurse
- basic and on-going education and training associated with appraisal and aimed at improving performance, changing unacceptable attitudes and up dating knowledge.

From the managers point of view, **training must be valid.** In the case of nurse training, at basic or post-basic levels, this means that the content of the training must be usable and must translate back to the job situation, so that it can be used in the same form in which it is taught. The situation where school training is abandoned when the learner arrives on the ward means that something is wrong and the questions to ask are:

● Are the learners being taught procedures in a way that is inappropriate to the ward situation?
● Have practices in clinical areas become slack and in need of improvement?

Wherever the fault lies, efforts **must** be made by senior staff to co-ordinate the academic with the practical. It is no longer acceptable to allow a disparity between what is known to be good practice and what, in fact, happens.

Nurses, attending training courses as part of post-basic training, may find that what they have learned and may wish to put into practice cannot be achieved. This is usually because their senior manager lacks a real interest in what takes place at the course, and is only concerned with being able to say that he or she has sent X number of nurses on Y courses as proof of the fact that he or she is carrying out the responsibility of training of staff. Even today, when the need to improve performance is vital for the career development of nurses, little care is given to:

● preparing a trainee for the course to be attended
● expecting the trainee to define his or her objectives in attending the course
● helping the trainee while on the course
● agreeing the possible changes that the trainee might make as its result
● monitoring the improvement in performance, the change in attitudes and the actual policies or procedures which the trainee has instituted following the course
● making available the resources the trainee may need to achieve these objectives.

From the trainee's point of view, improvements in performance as a result of training can only come about:

● if the trainee **wants** to improve (so he or she should not be 'sent' unwillingly for training)
● if the trainee is prepared to accept criticism and to face up to his or her own shortcomings
● if the training takes place in an environment where the trainee can look at these shortcomings without feeling threatened
● if the trainee trusts the trainer
● if the trainee is supported by his or her manager.

Good communication skills in management need constant care, constant review to ensure that a high standard is being maintained and the humility to accept that we all fail from time to time. As Somerset Maugham[2] said, 'We seek pitifully to convey to others the treasures of our heart, but they have not the power to accept them, and so we go lonely, side by side but not together, unable to know our fellows and unknown to them.'

References

1. Joanna Gray and Barbara Scammell, *Caring Communications Training Package* (Report to the NHS Training Authority, 1985).
2. Somerset Maugham, *The moon and sixpence* (Pan, 1975).

Index